LIVE FREE:
A 5-Week Devotional Journal for Students
(and anyone else who needs a little more grace in their lives)
Published by Orange
a division of The reThink Group, Inc.
5870 Charlotte Lane, Suite 300
Cumming, GA 30040 U.S.A.

Other Orange products are available online and direct from the publisher.

Visit www.OrangeBooks.com and www.ThinkOrange.com for more resources like these.

ISBN: 9781941259450

©2015 Ben Crawshaw and Jared Jones

Writers: Ben Crawshaw and Jared Jones
Lead Editors: Crystal Chiang and Steve Underwood
Editorial Team: Sara Shelton, Tim Walker, Mike Jeffries
Project Manager: Nate Brandt
Art Direction: Ryan Boon
Design: Hudson Phillips

Printed in the United States of America
First Edition 2015

2 3 4 5 6 7 8 9 10 11

06/26/2019

**Copies of this book are available for distribution in churches, schools,
and other venues at a significant quantity discount.
For more details, go to www.OrangeStore.org.**

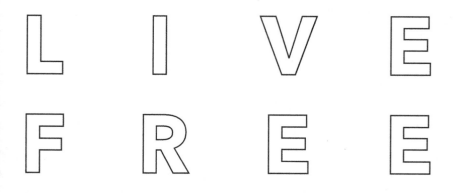

# LIVE FREE

## A 5-WEEK DEVOTIONAL JOURNAL FOR STUDENTS

### (AND ANYONE ELSE WHO NEEDS A LITTLE MORE GRACE IN THEIR LIVES)

**BEN CRAWSHAW & JARED JONES**

# INTRO-
# DUCTION

# CLIFF DIVING

**When you read or hear the word FREEDOM, what do you think about?**

Go ahead. Write it down. In fact, write all over this journal. Write anything—and anywhere—you want. This isn't a high school textbook (there will probably never be a textbook entitled *Live Free*). So grab a pen. Remember those? Little sticks that you used to write with before Siri typed everything for you? We tried to create a touch-screen journal with a virtual keyboard, but we couldn't afford it. We'll have to stick with old-school writing for now.

**SO WRITE DOWN THE FIRST THING THAT COMES TO MIND WHEN YOU THINK ABOUT FREEDOM.**

........................................................................................................

........................................................................................................

........................................................................................................

If that space isn't enough for your answer, feel free to get creative. Jot down a poem, draw a picture, or sketch a prototype that will make you millions of dollars one day (now *that* would be freedom).

When the word "freedom" hit your brain, maybe your mind went to something like this:

Or this:

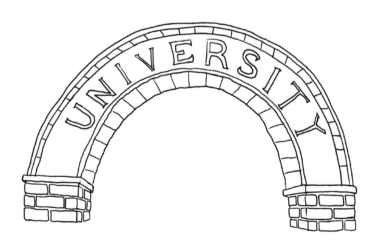

NOW, IF YOU COULD LIVE FREE, WHAT WOULD YOU **DO**? MAKE A LIST.

..................................................................................................

..................................................................................................

..................................................................................................

Would you do something like this?

Or this:

Okay, maybe you nearly had a panic attack thinking about snowboard backflips and cliff diving. For you, LIVING FREE might look more like this:

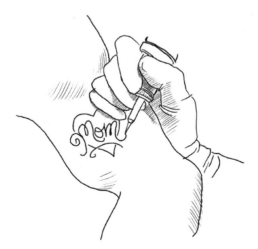

Or this:

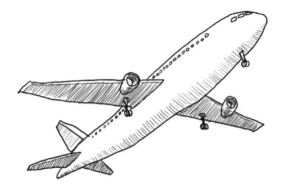

Maybe you'd move to a place like this:

Whatever came to mind, it probably made you happy, didn't it?

The truth is, when you're a teenager, FREEDOM is a great word.

Now, let's turn our attention away from cliff diving, tattoos, and tropical islands. Think about God. When it comes to your relationship with Him, how would you define FREEDOM? Don't write the answer that you think your mom, student pastor or small group leader wants you to give. Write your answer. From your heart and mind. Or feel free to draw a picture or write one of your favorite quotes or Bible verses. No one is going to grade your journal to make sure you have the right answers. So don't hold back. **WHAT WOULD REAL FREEDOM LOOK LIKE IN YOUR RELATIONSHIP WITH GOD?**

..................................................................................................................

..................................................................................................................

..................................................................................................................

**WHAT HOLDS YOU BACK FROM LIVING FREE IN YOUR RELATIONSHIP WITH GOD?**

..................................................................................................................

..................................................................................................................

..................................................................................................................

Ever heard of Paul from the Bible? If not, don't stress—we'll bring you up to speed in the next chapter. Paul was a guy who learned what it meant to live free in his relationship with God. And when he did...well, let's just say he went for it.

Like, backflip-off-a-cliff-into-tropical-waters went for it.

THE TRUTH
IS, WHEN
YOU'RE A
TEENAGER,
FREEDOM
IS A GREAT
WORD.

# WORLDWIDE RELIGION

**There are a lot of famous Pauls** (well, famous enough to have their own Wikipedia page):

- Paul McCartney
- Paul Revere
- Les Paul
- Paul Rudd
- Chris Paul
- Paul Walker
- Paul Kevin Jonas
- Sean Paul
- Paul Bunyan

But this journal is not about Paul McCartney. It's about the Apostle Paul. Why? Well for starters, you can't base a devotional journal on a guy who does a song with Kanye West and Rihanna. That's just wrong. Also because the Apostle Paul said and did some things that can have an impact on your life, right now.

Let's start by putting Paul's life in perspective. We often think of Christianity as a worldwide religion. That doesn't mean *everyone* is a Christian or that Christianity is *everywhere*. But it's definitely not some unknown religious cult.

This wasn't always the case. In fact, early in Christianity's history, all of the world's Christians were in one city: Jerusalem. And they were just a small group of Jews who believed that their leader, Jesus of Nazareth, was the Messiah who would save the world. They believed this even though Jesus had been publically humiliated and executed by the Roman government. Those early Christians held tightly to an insane belief that, even though He had been killed, Jesus *rose from the dead.*

It's easy for us to look back on those times and think, *"Ancient people had no concept of science. They would've believed anything. Of course they thought Jesus rose from the dead."* But their first response was actually the opposite. **They were so blindsided by His DEATH that they had zero ability to put faith in His RESURRECTION.** When people believe you're the Messiah, no one thinks you're going to be crucified on a cross and then buried in a tomb. When that happens, people conclude they must have been wrong about you.

And if they didn't expect the Messiah to die, then they *definitely* didn't expect Him to die and then, well, *un-die.* People at that time understood, like we do today, that *no one* comes back from the dead. Yet this small, dedicated group of people in Jerusalem held onto the impossible belief that their Messiah was alive. And then...

**Flash forward about 45 years and Christianity was now EVERYWHERE.** Believers were not only in Jerusalem, but all around the Mediterranean Region. Christianity was growing in Asia Minor (modern-day Turkey), Egypt, Greece, and even Rome. **Somehow, a small movement that should have faded away had grown into a worldwide religion.** It was growing so fast, in fact, that Roman politicians were taking notice and getting nervous. They began discussing how to deal with these pesky Christians who were popping up everywhere. What could've caused such a massive spread of a religion in such a short period of time?

**The short answer: God.**
**The longer answer: God used Paul.**

The even longer answer is that Paul was a pivotal part of the early spread of Christianity. He planted churches all throughout the known world at that time. Everywhere he went, Paul would start a church and tell people about Jesus.

Now, you may be thinking, *"Okay, so Paul was a pastor. Big deal. I don't know any pastor with a life that's crazy enough to deserve a big discussion."* First, your pastor probably has a crazier life than you realize. Second, Paul not only had a crazy life, he had a tough life.

We're talking really, really, really difficult.

Paul planted dozens of churches in places that didn't exactly welcome him with open arms. He was frequently slandered, imprisoned, and beaten. There were even numerous attempts to kill him. Think of a life that's more SEAL Team Six, less TV evangelist. In 2 Corinthians 11:23-25, Paul actually lists the trials he's faced:

> *"I am talking like a madman—with far greater labors, far more imprisonments, with countless beatings, and often near death. Five times I received at the hands of the Jews the forty lashes less one. Three times I was beaten with rods. Once I was stoned. Three times I was shipwrecked; a night and a day I was adrift at sea..."* (ESV)[1]

So let's review Paul's stats:

- He received around 195 lashes with a whip specially designed to rip out as much flesh as possible with each hit. Some people even died after one flogging. Paul took five in his lifetime.
- On three other occasions he was beaten with sticks and rods. Not fun.

- Once he was stoned. No, not the kind of stoned you're thinking. We're talking a bunch of men gathered around him with giant rocks. With both hands, they threw those rocks as hard as they could at Paul's head. It was like a really awful form of dodge ball.
- He was shipwrecked three times. Back then, if you got shipwrecked you couldn't call the US Coast Guard to have them rescue you. You had to find a way to survive. We're talking Tom Hanks in *Castaway*. (Wait, you've never heard of that movie? Never mind.)
- A night and day adrift at sea. One word: sharks.

Paul goes on to list all of the different places he faced danger:

> *"On frequent journeys, in danger from rivers, danger from robbers, danger from my own people, danger from Gentiles, danger in the city, danger in the wilderness, danger at sea, danger from false brothers; in toil and hardship, through many a sleepless night, in hunger and thirst, often without food, in cold and exposure. And, apart from other things, there is the daily pressure on me of my anxiety for all the churches[2]"*
> *(2 Corinthians 11:26-28 ESV).*

If you can't tell from this list, Paul was in danger *everywhere* he went. Not only that, he also carried the "daily pressure on me of my anxiety for all the churches." So add anxiety on top of beatings, stonings, and shipwreckings*.

Why would someone go through all of this? What was it that kept Paul going?

Before we answer that question, let's first back up to a different time, when Paul was a different person.

...........................................................................

[1]*Okay, we made up that word.*

In fact, he even had a different name. Granted, it was only different by one letter, but he was definitely a different person under that name. And he was not a fan of Christianity. In fact, he outright hated it.

# SAUL

If you knew Saul, you probably wouldn't have liked him. He was the ultimate rule follower and the most "by the book" person you could imagine. You may be a rule follower yourself. That's great. But I *promise* that you're not like Saul. He lived in Crazy Town at the intersection of Rule Following and Insanity.

Have you ever spent time with somebody who seemed to judge everything you said or did? That was Saul—Mr. Judgmental. You had to keep your guard up around him. Your behavior had to be near perfect. And if it wasn't, he'd let you know.

Did you ever have homework in elementary school? Did you ever forget to do it? (If not, just play along.) Imagine that your class is two minutes away from the dismissal bell, and your teacher still hasn't collected the assigned homework. You're throwing an internal party because you're convinced she forgot. And then. There's *that* Kid. You know…*him*. That guy who raises his hand to kindly remind the teacher to collect the assignment. Remember that kid? THAT was Saul.

Not only that, Saul was a racist and religious fanatic who hated everyone who didn't see things his way. He oversaw the persecution of some of his own countrymen because they believed differently than he did. At one point, he even held peoples' coats while they murdered a young Jewish man named Stephen, who was helping elderly widows in the local church.

How'd you like to have *that* guy hanging around?

Saul was seriously not someone you'd want to mess with. He wasn't even someone you'd want to talk to…ever. You would try to avoid him at all costs. And if you did cross paths, you made sure everything in your life was nice and tidy.

But Saul didn't hate people just for the sake of hating people. He wasn't a cranky old man who led an angry, lonely life. At this point he was actually a fairly young guy who truly believed that it was in people's best interests to follow the rules, and he was merely trying to help them do so. He was completely driven by his passion to impact the world. In fact, **Saul acted the way he did because of what he believed about God.** He saw God as a powerful deliverer who would one day rescue his people from the harsh rule of the Romans. Saul knew that God was righteous and holy. He knew that the rules mattered to God.

Like many religious people around him, Saul wondered why God still hadn't saved his people. What was taking so long? Maybe Saul guessed that God was waiting on His people to get their act together first. God's deliverance wasn't happening because the people of Israel weren't following the rules. Maybe Saul thought, *"If God's people would keep God's rules, then God would save them."* Seems logical, right?

Think of it in this extremely silly way. If your dog gets a treat when he sits, but he refuses to sit, wouldn't that be annoying? Of course it would. You'd think, *"Come on, Tsunami! Quit being an idiot and sit down!"* (By the way, Tsunami is a great name for a dog. So is Sasquatch. Or Thor.) But since Tsunami won't follow the rules, he can't get a treat. And that frustrates you.

That's why Saul was so vigilant. He figured God felt the same way about humans that you might feel about your disobedient dog. Saul's beliefs decided his actions. He only knew God as a judge, so Saul was quick to judge others. He only knew God as someone who punished sins, so Saul was quick to punish sins.

Make sense?

SAUL ACTED
THE WAY HE
DID BECAUSE
OF WHAT HE
BELIEVED
ABOUT GOD.

THEN, ONE DAY EVERYTHING CHANGED.
AND EVENTUALLY, SAUL BECAME PAUL.

Yes, *the* Apostle Paul.
You know, *the* guy who wrote most of the New Testament.

Now, if you could have met *Paul*, you probably would've loved him. Paul was a kind man who deeply loved those around him. He was honest and not afraid to speak his mind, but was also willing to admit his mistakes. He made no attempt to hide his less-than-perfect past. Paul knew what it meant to be a sinner, and even declared himself as the "worst of sinners." He was gentle with the broken, but firm with those who thought they had it all together. Paul was the farthest thing from a racist. He didn't think that non-Jews were dirty people. He didn't believe they were unable to receive God's love. He saw them as broken sinners desperately in need of something greater to help them.

PAUL WAS ALMOST THE EXACT OPPOSITE OF SAUL.

Where Saul reminded people of the ways they didn't measure up, Paul boldly announced that God loved people just as they were. While Saul was passionate about the Law, Paul was driven by grace.

So you have to ask yourself: **What caused Saul to become Paul?** What made him change his mind about almost everything he believed? What made him stop destroying churches and start planting them? The answer is the most common Sunday School answer of all time:

**Jesus.**

SAUL MET JESUS ON THE ROAD TO DAMASCUS AND IT CHANGED HIS UNDERSTANDING OF WHO GOD WAS.

**And when Saul's beliefs changed, everything in his life changed, too.**

Now, you may be thinking, *"This is a great history lesson, but what exactly does this have to do with me?"* Well, it actually has a lot to do with you. And me. If you think about it, our world isn't so different from Paul's world. Sure, we have things like the Internet, cars, football and Taylor Swift that weren't around when Paul was alive. But just like then, there are still plenty of people around who believe we have to shape up in order to get God to like us.

Some of us feel like God is a cosmic Santa Claus who's making His list and checking it twice. God makes us uncomfortable, and we feel like we need to have everything in order before we talk to Him.

Or, some of us act like God isn't concerned at all with how we live. We just say, "YOLO!" and try to occupy our time with whatever we can find, whether it's partying, boyfriends/girlfriends, video games or Netflix. We attempt to numb ourselves while we secretly wonder if our lives are going to amount to much.

Paul shows us something different. **Paul says that because of Jesus, we know that God is passionate about pursuing a relationship with us even when we don't have it all together.** Paul encourages us to stop trying to earn God's favor, to admit our failures, and to embrace the love and acceptance of Christ. Paul wants us to leave our inner Sauls at the door and be loved. He wants to let God's love change the way we live. Ultimately, PAUL INVITES US TO EXCHANGE RULES FOR RELATIONSHIP.

This journal is designed to take you on the same journey that Paul experienced, one that moves you toward Grace. Over the next few weeks, we'll explore Paul and his understanding of who God is, and we'll see how it connects to our world today. But before we start, you need to know something: **there's nothing you've done before picking up this book—and nothing you could do after you put down this book—that can change the way God feels about you.**

You are loved. You are invited to be part of God's Story. Not because of anything you've earned or anything you've done, but because of Jesus. Not only did you do nothing to earn His love, but you can do nothing to lose it. That's the mystery Paul discovered. It's called grace. It changed his life, and ultimately it changed the world. And it's available to you as well.

BECAUSE OF JESUS, PAUL LEARNED TO LIVE FREE.

# NO STRINGS ATTACHED

Just to practice living free—and to warm you up to the idea of getting other people involved in this journey—we want you to do something a little silly.

**Tear out the slips on the next page and give one to five different people.** It's a simple request for them to give you something for free.

Here's the catch: There is no catch. You're asking for no-strings-attached gifts. Whether it's dental floss, duct tape or a twenty-dollar bill, you can't do anything to earn it. You may not get great stuff, but it *will* be free. And it's important to get the idea of FREE in your mind.

PLEASE GIVE ME
SOMETHING FREE

PLEASE GIVE ME
SOMETHING FREE

PLEASE GIVE ME
SOMETHING FREE

PLEASE GIVE ME
SOMETHING FREE

PLEASE GIVE ME
SOMETHING FREE

WRITE DOWN WHAT YOU COLLECTED.

1.
.......................................................................................

.......................................................................................

2.
.......................................................................................

.......................................................................................

3.
.......................................................................................

.......................................................................................

4.
.......................................................................................

.......................................................................................

5.
.......................................................................................

.......................................................................................

# WEEK ONE: WHO IS JESUS?

**Saul was on a mission.**

His goal: to root out followers of Jesus, the so-called "Messiah," in Jerusalem. But now it was time to expand his operation, so he set his eyes on the city of Damascus. His Damascus to-do list consisted of two things:

1. Find Christians.
2. Convince them not to be Christians.

"Convince" is such a nice way to phrase it. Just like the mafia "convinces" people to hand over money they owe. Saul traveled with his gang of religious thugs to eradicate people who worshipped a Man he had never met.

Saul had heard rumors of this "Jesus" character—a hippie, a free spirit, and a teacher who loved everyone, including tax collectors. (And what kind of person could possibly love tax collectors?!) Supposedly, Jesus even loved common criminals who were executed by the Romans. None of that sounded very Messiah-like.

But these crazy Christians continued to claim that Jesus was the Messiah. Even crazier, they said that Jesus had risen from the dead. Saul probably thought they were insane. So he decided that the only remedy to this insanity was to show them just how wrong they were. *Someone* had to maintain order.

But on the way to Damascus, Saul encountered something he didn't expect. As he traveled north from Jerusalem, Saul collided with someone who would change his life forever. And not only change the course of his life, but the course of the entire world.

That day, Saul came face to face with Jesus.

*Meanwhile, Saul was still breathing out murderous threats against the Lord's disciples. He went to the high priest and asked him for letters to the synagogues in Damascus, so that if he found any there who belonged to the Way, whether men or women, he might take them as prisoners to Jerusalem. As he neared Damascus on his journey, suddenly a light from heaven flashed around him. He fell to the ground and heard a voice say to him, "Saul, Saul, why do you persecute me?"*

*"Who are you, Lord?' Saul asked.*

*"I am Jesus, whom you are persecuting," he replied. "Now get up and go into the city, and you will be told what you must do."*

*The men traveling with Saul stood there speechless; they heard the sound but did not see anyone. Saul got up from the ground, but when he opened his eyes he could see nothing. So they led him by the hand into Damascus. For three days he was blind, and did not eat or drink anything. (Acts 9:1-9).*

Up to this point in the church's early history, Saul was the main villain in the story. The ultimate bad guy. Later in Saul's life (after he became Paul), he said that of every sinner in the entire world, he was "the worst of them all."

When we think of "sin," we often think of different things we do that are bad: drinking, drugs, partying, lying, sex, disrespecting authority or whatever else we label as wrong. You may read this and think, *I know exactly who is the worst sinner in the world. I go to school with him or her.* Or you may think, *I'm pretty sure I am the worst sinner I know!*

Sin is about more than our actions. It's something inside us. In Romans, Paul describes it as our sin *nature*. Because we're human beings, we have a nature that separates us from God. At its root, sin nature is *a deeply held allegiance to something other than Jesus.* So Saul considered himself the chief sinner because he was once chief enemy to Jesus and the Church.

But here's the amazing news: Saul was an enemy of Jesus in *his* mind. But Jesus thought something entirely different. Jesus loved Saul. And Jesus wanted to save Saul. Here's the rest of the verse:

> **This is a trustworthy saying, and everyone should accept it: "Christ Jesus came into the world to save sinners[3]"— and I am the worst of them all (1 Timothy 1:15 NLT).**

Jesus came into the world to save sinners, including those who hated Him. He came to save people who were born with a sinful nature that placed a wall between them and God. Jesus went beyond just saving us from our sins—He saved us from ourselves.

Saul deserved God's judgement. But instead he received God's mercy. Jesus loved Saul even when Saul hated Jesus. That's grace. And this act of grace stayed with him the rest of his life. It changed his beliefs, his behaviors, and even his name!

Okay, back to the story.

When he encountered Jesus, Saul didn't know *who* He was, but he knew *what* He was: *"Who are you, Lord?"* What an amazing statement! It shows two things.

First, Saul didn't know the correct answers. Saul didn't "figure out" his way into faith. He still had questions. In fact, the whole Jesus situation just got a lot more confusing. Because up to this moment, Saul had assumed God was on his side. God would be proud of him for murdering all these cultists called Christians. Then, suddenly everything changed. Saul realized—to his horror—that he had actually been persecuting *God* all along.

The second thing we learn is that Saul did nothing to earn God's grace. It's not like Saul suddenly felt empathetic while he was torturing a Christian and decided to change his ways. No, Jesus showed up while Saul was on the road to imprison and kill even more Christians. Paul did nothing good to deserve it. On that road, God had mercy on Saul, purely because God decided to have mercy on him.

That's important for you to know. Why? Because you didn't do anything to earn God's grace, either. In fact, you can't do anything do deserve it. In almost every dictionary, "grace" is defined as *unmerited or undeserved favor from God.* That means you *can't* earn it. **GRACE IS GETTING WHAT YOU DON'T DESERVE. ONCE SOMETHING IS EARNED, IT'S NO LONGER GRACE. YOU CAN'T DO ANYTHING TO "QUALIFY" FOR IT. THAT'S WHY SO MANY PEOPLE DESCRIBE GRACE AS "AMAZING."**

The drama continues in Acts 9:

> *In Damascus there was a disciple named Ananias. The Lord called to him in a vision, "Ananias!"*
>
> *"Yes, Lord," he answered.*
>
> *The Lord told him, "Go to the house of Judas on Straight Street and ask for a man from Tarsus named Saul, for he is praying. In a vision he has seen a man named Ananias come and place his hands on him to restore his sight."*
>
> *"Lord," Ananias answered, "I have heard many reports about this man and all the harm he has done to your*

GRACE IS
GETTING
WHAT YOU
DON'T
DESERVE.
ONCE
SOMETHING
IS EARNED,
IT'S NO
LONGER
GRACE.

*holy people in Jerusalem. And he has come here with authority from the chief priests to arrest all who call on your name."*

*But the Lord said to Ananias, "Go! This man is my chosen instrument to proclaim my name to the Gentiles and their kings and to the people of Israel. I will show him how much he must suffer for my name."*

*Then Ananias went to the house and entered it. Placing his hands on Saul, he said, "Brother Saul, the Lord— Jesus, who appeared to you on the road as you were coming here—has sent me so that you may see again and be filled with the Holy Spirit." Immediately, something like scales fell from Saul's eyes, and he could see again. He got up and was baptized, and after taking some food, he regained his strength (Acts 9:10-19).*

Picture a normal guy hanging out in Damascus. He's heard rumors that Saul—the ultimate bad guy—is coming up from Jerusalem to terrorize Christians. All of a sudden, God appears to him in a vision. *That alone* is pretty crazy. But then God starts a somewhat comical conversation with him. Maybe it went something like this:

GOD: "Hey Ananias, Saul is in town. No, no, no, *I don't* want you to hide from him. Actually, here's where he's staying. I want you to go talk to him."

ANANIAS: "Hang on, I think you're breaking up. I must have misheard you. You want me to *what?*"

GOD: "You heard me. I want you to go talk to him. Don't worry, I already let him know you are coming."

ANANIAS: "Maybe there's more than one Saul. You're probably talking about some nice farmer named Saul, right? Not the scary-guy Saul."

GOD: "No, I'm talking about Saul, the guy who persecutes Christians."

ANANIAS: "I know that You see *everything*. But as a quick refresher, you know that I *am* a Christian, don't you?"

GOD: "Yup."

ANANIAS: "My point is that it doesn't seem like the best idea for me to go find the man who is here for the sole purpose of ruining my life."

GOD: "Ananias, I understand you're afraid. But trust me, I've got big plans for Saul. He's *my* guy, and he's going to change the world for *my* sake. And just so you know, it's going to cost him EVERYTHING—even his life. So go help the guy, please!"

ANANIAS: "Okay. Uh, run that address by me one more time?"

Maybe that's not *exactly* how it went down. But you get the idea. It's such an amazing picture of grace in action! Jesus shows Saul grace by showing up. Then Christians, like Ananias, begin to show Saul grace, too.

In the end, the road to Damascus was the location where Saul realized that he had been an enemy to Jesus, the Son of God. And he realized that Jesus loved him anyway.

Saul's encounter with Jesus would forever shape his life and destiny. And the theme of that encounter was amazing grace.

From that day forward, Saul was becoming Paul.

# DAY ONE
## LOWERING THE BAR

Let's talk about dating.

Your favorite topic.

Are you currently dateless but wishing that weren't the case? Are you currently dating someone but wishing you weren't? Is dating a regret from your past? A hope for your future? Something your mom won't stop bugging you about?

Here's another question: what are your standards for the person you date?

- Good looking?
- Nice?
- A Christian?
- Breathing?
- Athletic and muscular?
- Artistic and mysterious?
- Funny?
- Serious?
- A guy with a beard?
- A girl without a beard?
- Cat lover?
- Cat hater?
- Smart but humble?
- Stupid but nice?

The truth is, even if you've never thought about it, you probably have *some* type of standard when it comes to the person you date. Even if that standard is as low as "must have all their teeth" or "can't currently be in jail," you've probably set the bar *somewhere*.

In the same way—even if it's in the back of your mind—**you probably have a standard for how you think Christians should talk and behave.** Whether you feel like you fall well below that bar, or whether you feel like you *are* the bar, you probably have a standard.

**WHAT'S THE STANDARD THAT YOU THINK CHRISTIANS *SHOULD* LIVE UP TO?**

......................................................................................

......................................................................................

......................................................................................

Do you live up to that same standard? The truth is, no matter how good you are, you have your moments, don't you? Your selfish moments. Your secret moments. Your stupid moments.

Then what?

**WHAT DO YOU TYPICALLY SAY TO YOURSELF WHEN YOU FALL SHORT OF THAT STANDARD?**

......................................................................................

......................................................................................

......................................................................................

That's the moment when you have to decide what you think about grace. But first, let's define it.

**DEFINE GRACE.**

..................................................................................

..................................................................................

..................................................................................

Now, let's go beyond just writing a definition. **WRITE ABOUT A TIME IN YOUR LIFE WHEN YOU EXPERIENCED GRACE.**

..................................................................................

..................................................................................

..................................................................................

Back in the day, did you ever watch *The Oprah Winfrey Show?* (Of course you didn't—you weren't a 40-year-old housewife.) Oprah loves to give stuff away. For example, one time everyone in the audience got a new car. Another time she gave each person a trip to Disney World. What did they do to earn that car or that trip to Disney? Nothing. They showed up.

That's grace.

Here's an obvious question: Do you think those audience members became bigger fans of Oprah? Of course they did! We'd be raving fans of anyone who gave us a new ride and a free vacation.

That's what grace does. It makes us bigger Jesus fans. Because we realize that we don't deserve—and we didn't earn—His love, favor, acceptance and compassion.

**SPEND A FEW MINUTES THANKING GOD FOR ALL THE WAYS HE'S SHOWN YOU GRACE.**

# DAY TWO
## GRACE UNDER FIRE

Have your parents ever hired an exterminator to come to your house? Some guy who showed up wearing a helmet because... well, we actually have *no idea* why exterminators wear helmets. Maybe they're dealing with some pretty huge termites? Or maybe the termites are just really angry and want to fight? Anyway, the exterminator spent four minutes spraying some kind of liquid in the corners of your house and then handed over a bill for $150. Not bad for a few minutes of work, huh?

Exterminators have one primary job: to eliminate pests.

That's what Saul was—an exterminator. One of the definitions of persecute is "to exterminate people based on their membership in a religious, ethnic, social or racial group." Saul viewed Christians as pests. And he viewed himself as the go-to termite guy.

Then Saul had a mind-blowing encounter with Jesus on a dusty road. And Jesus asked him, quite simply, *"Saul, Saul, why are you persecuting Me?"* Wait. Saul had never persecuted JESUS when JESUS was on earth. Saul had never even met Him.

But Saul *had* persecuted Jesus' followers. And Jesus was saying, "What my people go through, I go through. Those who follow Me don't *just* follow Me. We're in a relationship. We're close. We are united. When you persecute THEM, you persecute ME."

What does that mean for you? It means that when you go through tough stuff—although it may not be persecution—God cares. He knows what you're going through. He feels what you're feeling.

**NAME ONE OR TWO DIFFICULT THINGS YOU'RE DEALING WITH RIGHT NOW.**

.................................................................................................................

.................................................................................................................

.................................................................................................................

Later on in his life, when Paul had a much better understanding of both who God is and what difficult situations really look like, he said,

> *"For I am convinced that neither death nor life, neither angels nor demons, neither the present nor the future, nor any powers, neither height nor depth, nor ANYTHING else in all creation, will be able to separate us from the love of God that is in Christ Jesus our Lord"* *(Romans 8:38-39 emphasis added).*

Paul knew this: when he went through tough times, God was there with him. Right in the middle of it. Nothing could separate Paul from the love of God.

The same is true for you. When you face life's storms, God is with you. He is ALWAYS there. He is with you whether you think you deserve it or not. That's grace.

If you're on a boat in the middle of a windy storm, an anchor can keep your boat from rolling, help it steer in the right direction, and reduce the distance that it can drift. Anchors offer stability. **The idea of never being separated from Jesus was Paul's anchor.**

*You need an anchor phrase to hold on to when you face life's storms.*

WRITE DOWN AN ANCHOR PHRASE YOU CAN HOLD ON TO IN TOUGH TIMES—SOMETHING THAT WILL REMIND YOU THAT GOD IS WITH YOU.

................................................................................

................................................................................

................................................................................

SPEND A FEW MINUTES PRAYING. BE HONEST WITH GOD ABOUT WHAT YOU'RE DEALING WITH. THEN SAY YOUR ANCHOR PHRASE (OUT LOUD IF YOU CAN) SEVERAL TIMES. MEMORIZE IT SO YOU CAN HOLD ONTO IT WHEN YOU NEED TO.

# DAY THREE
## GREAT EPECTATIONS

She may not make a regular appearance on your Spotify rotation, but you've probably heard of Adele. She's won ten Grammys and about a billion other awards.

But did you know that she has major stage fright? At one show in Amsterdam, Adele was so nervous that she snuck out of an emergency exit before her show. She's thrown up multiple times before taking the stage. Adele even said that "Once in Brussels, I projectile-vomited on someone."[4] We're talking about an artist whose net worth is *$55 million!* Imagine the Belgian fan who showed up to see one of today's most famous artists only to be hurled on by that artist.

One word: lawsuit. Make that vomit pay!

Seriously, though, I bet that fan had an entirely different expectation for Adele's concert. And those expectations were, um, hurled out the window*.

The truth is, we all have expectations for how we think things are going to be.

Saul had an expectation of what God was like. He had spent his entire life devoted to who he thought God was. And his thinking led him to believe that Jesus—and anyone who followed Him—was a pretender. On his way to eliminate as many of those

* That's our last pun. For a while, anyway.

pretenders as possible, Saul's view of God and Jesus was flipped upside down by a blinding light and a voice from heaven.

*"I am Jesus, whom you are persecuting."*

"Uhhhh, what? Ohhhh, got it!"

Suddenly, Saul realized that he had been seeing God in the wrong light. God was different than he had ever expected.

But what happened next? Surely the next words out of God's mouth would be, "You idiot! What are you thinking? Do you realize all the damage you've done—all the people you've hurt? And all in *MY* name!"

Maybe that's what Saul expected. **WE ALL HAVE AN IDEA, AN EXPECTATION OF HOW WE** *THINK* **GOD SHOULD RESPOND TO ALL THE MESSED UP STUFF IN OUR LIVES.**

But instead of yelling at Saul, God simply says, "Go to Damascus."

**GOD DIDN'T BEAT SAUL UP. INSTEAD, HE JUST SHOWED SAUL HIS NEXT STEP.**

That's grace.

God wasn't who Saul thought He was. And God showed His true character by not responding the way Saul thought He would.

**WHAT DO YOU THINK GOD IS LIKE? (Try to use at least 5 non-churchy words to describe Him).**

........................................................................................................

........................................................................................................

WHAT DO YOU THINK GOD THINKS ABOUT YOU?

..............................................................................................

..............................................................................................

..............................................................................................

HOW DO YOU THINK GOD RESPONDS WHEN YOU MESS UP?

..............................................................................................

..............................................................................................

..............................................................................................

Just like Saul, God has a next step for you, too. God has a different version of "Get up and go to Damascus" for you.

TAKE A FEW MINUTES TO PRAY. OPEN UP WITH GOD. BE HONEST ABOUT ALL OF THE MESSED UP STUFF IN YOUR LIFE. INVITE HIM TO SHOW YOU THE WAYS HE'S NOT LIKE YOU'VE EXPECTED.

THEN, ASK HIM TO SHOW YOU THE NEXT SIMPLE STEP YOU'RE SUPPOSED TO TAKE. WHEN HE SHOWS YOU THAT STEP, WRITE IT HERE.

..............................................................................................

..............................................................................................

..............................................................................................

# DAY FOUR
## LOST CAUSE

Have you ever heard of the *Rocky* movies? They're centered on a boxer named—wait for it—Rocky. The films are all modern-day classics. I promise that you've at least heard the theme song at some point in your life.

*Rocky* was written by an actor named Sylvester Stallone. Rumor has it that Stallone saw a Muhammad Ali fight and then wrote the script over the next three days. The first movie was nominated for ten Academy Awards. According to one reviewer, Rocky is "one of the greatest, if not *the* greatest, feel-good movies of all time."[5]

But.

At the time Stallone wrote *Rocky*, he was a struggling actor working two jobs: one at a local deli and another as a movie theater usher. Can you imagine ordering a turkey pastrami sandwich from an actor who made such little money from, you know, *acting* that he had to work two other jobs to pay the rent? Let's say you struck up a conversation about his dreams and he told you, "I just wrote a screenplay that will be nominated for ten Academy Awards and become one of the greatest movies of all time."

Yeah. Right.

That's probably how Ananias felt after God told him to be prayer partners with Saul. It doesn't matter how great Saul *could* be one day. At that moment, he was a murderer. And for Ananias, that was probably a scary thought.

*"Lord," Ananias answered, "I have heard many reports about this man and all the harm he has done to your holy people in Jerusalem" (Acts 9:13).*

If Sylvester Stallone's rise to fame was a surprise, Saul's conversion was a mind-blowing miracle. But that's what God does—He goes above and beyond our view of what's possible. He surprises us with grace.

But here's something you need to know: **GOD'S GRACE ISN'T JUST *FOR* US. IT ALSO MOVES *THROUGH* US TO OTHER PEOPLE.**

If we're honest, we can all admit that we see some people as lost causes. And often for good reason. **WHAT WE *CAN'T* SEE IS WHAT CAN HAPPEN WHEN GOD ENTERS THEIR STORY.** We don't know what God has planned for their future. And we don't know the ways God could be moving in their lives.

God may be surprising them with grace. And He may have a part for us to play in the surprise party.

**WHAT ARE SOME WAYS YOU CAN SHOW GRACE TO UNLIKELY PEOPLE?**

.................................................................................................

.................................................................................................

.................................................................................................

WHY IS PRAYING FOR OTHER PEOPLE AND THEIR FUTURE AN
ACT OF GRACE?

.......................................................................................................

.......................................................................................................

.......................................................................................................

THINK OF TWO OR THREE PEOPLE WHO SEEM LIKE A LOST
CAUSE IN YOUR MIND. PRAY THAT GOD WILL GO BEYOND
HUMAN EXPECTATIONS AND REVEAL HIS GRACE TO THEM.
TELL GOD THAT YOU'RE READY TO BE PART OF THAT PLAN.

.......................................................................................................

.......................................................................................................

.......................................................................................................

# DAY FIVE
## RICH RELATIVE

The Eastern European country Moldova is beautiful, but it's certainly not wealthy. In fact, it is Europe's poorest nation.[6]

Enter Sergey Sudev, a journalism student in Moldova. Sudev was working at a local radio station when he found out he had just inherited a fortune from a distant uncle in Germany that he hadn't seen in ten years.[7]

The amount? Let's just say it tipped the $1 billion scale! And just like that, Sudev became one of the richest human beings in his entire country.

Sudev thought it was a joke. Wouldn't you? But then representatives for his uncle's estate confirmed the money was now his.

No joke, Sergey.

That's what grace is like—a billion-dollar inheritance. You can see it as a joke, a scam, as too good to be true. You can turn it away, claiming that you don't deserve it and didn't earn it.

Or you can receive it.

If you grew up in church, you've probably heard someone say, "Jesus loves you." Maybe you sang those words in a song. Maybe you've said that phrase to someone else. But **THERE'S A DIFFERENCE BETWEEN HEARING ABOUT GRACE AND *BELIEVING* IN IT. THERE'S A DIFFERENCE BETWEEN SINGING ABOUT IT AND RECEIVING IT.**

**WHY IS IT DIFFICULT TO BELIEVE IN AND RECEIVE GOD'S GRACE FOR YOU?**

........................................................................................

........................................................................................

........................................................................................

**WHAT WOULD YOU DO DIFFERENTLY IF YOU WERE 100% SURE GOD LOVED YOU NO MATTER WHAT? HOW WOULD YOU THINK DIFFERENTLY?**

........................................................................................

........................................................................................

........................................................................................

When Saul believed in and received grace, he began to live differently. He began to live free. It launched him on a mission to declare that message to as many people as possible. In fact, we're still talking about grace today because Saul encountered grace.

Believe it. Receive it. Own it. Personalize it. Embrace it. Declare it. Think it.

**SPEND A FEW MINUTES PRAYING. ASK GOD TO HELP YOU BELIEVE AND RECEIVE HIS GRACE TOWARD YOU.**

# WEEK TWO: CAN I TRUST GOD?

**Hype ruins everything.** *Everything.* Think about the last time someone told you about a concert, a new band, even a new app, and they really hyped it up. Weren't you ultimately disappointed when you finally experienced it for yourself? Maybe you went to a restaurant with your buddy because he wouldn't shut up about the fish tacos. He would offer rave reviews like, *"they're literally the greatest things you will ever eat in your entire life!"* By the time you finally taste these life-changing tacos, you're not all that impressed. It's not that they're bad—they're just not as good as your buddy made them out to be.

Or maybe your friend tells you that you just *have* to see the new Tom Cruise movie. I mean, the trailer was awesome so it has to be the greatest movie of all time, right? (Spoiler alert: Tom's character saves the world.) So you drag yourself to the movie, sit through two hours of explosions, and find yourself a little underwhelmed. The movie was fine—it just didn't live up to the hype.

This happens a lot, doesn't it? It's a rare event when something lives up to the hype surrounding it. Because of that, most of us probably have a little skepticism about anything that's saddled with a lot of hype.

Now here's a different question: Have you ever felt that way about God? You've heard all these things about Him—who He is and what He can do—and you've found yourself wondering if it could possibly be true. How could He ever live up to all the hype?

A lot of first-century Jews had the very same questions. But to get ourselves into the right mindset (meaning, we have to think like a first-century Jew), let's replace the word "hype" with the word "promises." In their time, there were a lot of *promises* made about God—some even coming from God Himself. Promises that He would save His people. Promises that He would right all wrongs. Promises that He would change the world.

Think about that for a second. How many things do you see that are wrong in our world today? How many people do you think need saving? How many things need to be changed? And God was telling the Jewish people, *"I can fix ALL of that!"* Talk about a lot of hype.

So how did they know that God could live up to it? How did they know whether or not He would actually deliver on those promises—that He would show up?

MAYBE THE REAL QUESTION FOR THEM (AND FOR US) IS THIS: HOW DO WE KNOW WE CAN TRUST GOD?

Paul absolutely believed that God was worth all of the hype. He knew without a doubt that God was going to deliver on all His promises. He knew that God was trustworthy. Paul described this confidence in God in a speech he gave at a Jewish synagogue in Antioch Pisidia:

> *Paul and his companions then left Paphos by ship for Pamphylia, landing at the port town of Perga. There John Mark left them and returned to Jerusalem. But Paul and Barnabas traveled inland to Antioch of Pisidia.*
>
> *On the Sabbath they went to the synagogue for the services. After the usual readings from the books of Moses and the prophets, those in charge of the service sent them this message: "Brothers, if you have any word of encouragement for the people, come and give it.*
>
> *So Paul stood, lifted his hand to quiet them, and started speaking. "Men of Israel," he said, "and you God-fearing Gentiles, listen to me. The God of this nation of Israel chose our ancestors and made them multiply and grow strong during their stay in Egypt. Then with a powerful arm he led them out of their slavery. He put up with*

*them through forty years of wandering in the wilderness.
Then he destroyed seven nations in Canaan and gave
their land to Israel as an inheritance. All this took about
450 years.*

*After that, God gave them judges to rule until the time
of Samuel the prophet. Then the people begged for a
king, and God gave them Saul son of Kish, a man of the
tribe of Benjamin, who reigned for forty years. But God
removed Saul and replaced him with David, a man about
whom God said, 'I have found David son of Jesse, a man
after my own heart. He will do everything I want him
to do.'*

*And it is one of King David's descendants, Jesus, who is
God's promised Savior of Israel!* [8]*" (Acts 13:13-23 NLT).*

Basically, Paul is asked to give a "word of encouragement" in the
synagogue after a time of morning worship. So he stands up and
starts recounting a brief history of the Jewish race. He focuses on
David.* He ends the first part of his speech by telling his audience
that Jesus is the Savior they had been promised—and he came
from the line of David.

This part was a big deal to them. When David was chosen as
the king of Israel, God promised him that there would always
be a king from David's lineage on Israel's throne. He promised
David that his dynasty would be eternal. But then David died.
And after that, his sons died. And for a long time there was no
king in Israel at all. So had God failed to come through on His
promise to David?

According to Paul, the answer is no—Jesus was the fulfillment of
the promise! Paul continues:

........................................................................................

*Remember King David? The guy who killed the giant Goliath with a sling and a stone? No? Go look him
up. We'll wait.*

*"Brothers—you sons of Abraham, and also you God-fearing Gentiles—this message of salvation has been sent to us! The people in Jerusalem and their leaders did not recognize Jesus as the one the prophets had spoken about. Instead, they condemned him, and in doing this they fulfilled the prophets' words that are read every Sabbath. They found no legal reason to execute him, but they asked Pilate to have him killed anyway.*

*"When they had done all that the prophecies said about him, they took him down from the cross and placed him in a tomb. But God raised him from the dead! And over a period of many days he appeared to those who had gone with him from Galilee to Jerusalem. They are now his witnesses to the people of Israel.*

*"And now we are here to bring you this Good News. The promise was made to our ancestors, and God has now fulfilled it for us, their descendants, by raising Jesus"* (Acts 13:26-33a).

Notice particularly what Paul says in verses 32 and 33: *"And we bring you the GOOD NEWS that what God promised to the fathers, this he has fulfilled to us their children by raising Jesus..."*

The phrase "good news" comes from the same Greek word that we often see translated into the word "Gospel" today. The Gospel—the story of Jesus' life, death, and resurrection—is the good news that **GOD HAS FULFILLED HIS PROMISES**.

And why is this good news? Because it forever answers a huge question: can we trust God? According to Paul, JESUS' LIFE, DEATH, AND RESURRECTION PROVE HE IS TRUSTWORTHY. HE IS WHO HE SAYS HE IS. HE WILL DO WHAT HE SAYS HE WILL DO.

JESUS' LIFE, DEATH, AND RESURRECTION PROVE HE IS TRUSTWORTHY. HE IS WHO HE SAYS HE IS. HE WILL DO WHAT HE SAYS HE WILL DO. HE IS WORTH ALL THE HYPE.

Later on in Paul's ministry, he puts it like this:

> *"For all the promises of God find their Yes in him[9]"*
> *(2 Corinthians 1:20 ESV).*

What an incredible thought! ALL THE PROMISES OF GOD ARE
ANSWERED WITH A "YES" BECAUSE OF JESUS.

Before Jesus, there were still a lot of questions about if and when
God would come through on His promises. God had generated
a lot of hype about saving His people, ruling the world, and
conquering sin and death. After a while, however, the silence
made it awkward for everyone. It was hard to believe that God
would do anything when He seemed to be doing nothing. For the
Jews, it began to feel like a lost cause.

But then came Jesus. And Jesus fulfilled all of those lofty promises
made by God. I mean, He rose from the dead! If that's not a
guarantee that God is legit, I don't know what it is! His life proved
that God is faithful to His word.

You may be thinking, *"Well, that's all great, but what does this
have to do with my life right now?"*

So glad you asked! Here's what this means for you: YOU CAN
TRUST HIM. It's as simple as that.

God is exactly who He promises He is. He doesn't make claims
about Himself that He can't deliver on. It isn't just a bunch of talk.
He follows through. Every. Single. Time.

So if He promised to never leave us, then He'll never leave us. If
He promised that we're forgiven, then we're forgiven.

Think about it in a personal way:

- If God promised He'd be with you through your parents' divorce, then He *really* is with you, even when it feels like He isn't.
- If God promised that He doesn't hold your sins against you, then your biggest sins aren't making Him turn his back on you, even if you feel that way.

God comes through on His promises. That's the Gospel. He lives up to all the hype. He's faithful to all His promises. Just wait and see.

# DAY ONE
## ALL-STARS

Can you name any professional athletes? Do you have a favorite? It's pretty remarkable when an athlete turns pro in any sport.

Now imagine when they can play two pro sports at the same time.

Deion Sanders not only played two sports, he had two nicknames—ridiculous, right? He was called "Prime Time" and "Neon Deion." He's the only man to play in both the Super Bowl and the World Series, and he's the only man ever to hit a home run and score a touchdown as a professional in the same week.

Bo Jackson also played football and baseball. He's the only athlete to be named an All-Star in two major sports. He was named ESPN's greatest athlete of all time.

But sports all-stars aren't just guys. Let's talk about Babe Didrikson. She won 41 LPGA events in golf, was an All-American college basketball player and won two track and field gold medals.

You can rattle off these stats if a coach ever pressures you to play only one sport.

Before Jesus showed up, people thought that only one team mattered: the Jewish people. All of the focus was on them. But when Paul gave his speech in Antioch, he made it clear that God was available to both the Jews and the Gentiles (non-Jews):

*"Brothers—you sons of Abraham, and also you God-fearing
Gentiles—this message of salvation has been sent to us!* [10]*"
(Acts 13:26 NLT).*

Us. As in, ALL of us. How? Why? Jesus, that's how and why.
*". . .through this man Jesus there is forgiveness for your sins* [11]*"
(Acts 13:38 NLT).*

JESUS IS WHAT MAKES ALL THE DIFFERENCE. That's why
Christians are all about Him. That's why entering into a
relationship with God happens only through faith and trust in the
person of Jesus. His death, burial, and resurrection are what make
forgiveness of sins possible for us.

SOMETIMES WE'RE STILL TEMPTED TO THINK THE MESSAGE OF
JESUS IS ONLY FOR CERTAIN KINDS OF PEOPLE. WHICH GROUPS
ARE YOU MOST TEMPTED TO THINK OF AS "DISQUALIFIED" TO
BE JESUS FOLLOWERS?

........................................................................................................

........................................................................................................

........................................................................................................

HOW IS YOUR LIFE DIFFERENT BECAUSE YOU WERE INCLUDED
IN THE MESSAGE OF JESUS?

........................................................................................................

........................................................................................................

........................................................................................................

SPEND A FEW MINUTES THANKING GOD FOR SENDING JESUS, MAKING IT POSSIBLE FOR YOUR SINS TO BE FORGIVEN, AND PROVIDING A WAY FOR YOU TO HAVE A RELATIONSHIP WITH GOD. ASK HIM TO HELP YOU SEE ALL PEOPLE AS HE SEES THEM.

# DAY TWO
## MARKED

Did you know that you can get a temporary tattoo by Mother Nature? No, we're not talking about pimples. We're talking about lightning flowers. It sounds really cool until you realize just *how* you receive this tattoo. You need to be on the receiving end of a lightning bolt.

When some (unfortunate) people get struck by lightning, they develop what are called "Lichtenberg Figures" across their skin.

In 2000, there was a medical report about a 54-year-old man who was struck by lightning. He felt fine, but doctors soon discovered a crazy leaf pattern across his arm, back and leg. The marks disappeared just two days later.

Medical experts determined that this skin pattern was likely caused by capillaries rupturing beneath the skin, as a result of the electrical discharge.[12]

So you can add that to your arsenal for trivia night.

You too are marked by something when you put your faith in Jesus. Here's how Paul described it:

*"For God had promised to raise him from the dead, not leaving him to rot in the grave. He said, 'I will give you the sacred blessings I promised to David'"[13]*
*(Acts 13:34 NLT).*

Because of Jesus, your life can be marked by **BLESSINGS** like:
- The unbreakable love of God
- A joyful life with God
- Peace with God

LIST SOME WAYS THAT GOD HAS BLESSED YOU.

...................................................................................................

...................................................................................................

HOW WOULD YOUR LIFE BE DIFFERENT IF YOU TRULY BELIEVED THAT GOD'S LOVE FOR YOU IS UNBREAKABLE?

...................................................................................................

...................................................................................................

...................................................................................................

IF YOU ACCEPTED THE FACT THAT YOU HAVE PEACE WITH GOD THROUGH JESUS, HOW WOULD YOU *THINK* DIFFERENTLY?

...................................................................................................

...................................................................................................

...................................................................................................

SPEND A FEW MINUTES PRAYING. INVITE GOD'S LOVE, PEACE, AND JOY INTO YOUR HEART AND MIND. ASK HIM TO HELP YOU THINK AND BELIEVE LIKE SOMEONE WHO HAS BEEN MARKED BY HIS BLESSINGS.

# DAY THREE
## SURVIVAL KIT

.................................................................................

Have you ever wanted to climb Mount Everest? Is there some part of you that says, "Yes, I'd love to experience a 40-day, life-endangering, 30,000-foot climb?" (We'd probably take a lightning flower over that ordeal.) If you're interested in taking on Everest, you need to be ready for a few inconveniences like freezing temps, high winds, and mental fatigue.*

The key to surviving the climb is preparation. In addition to physical training, you need to show up supplied with, well, *supplies.* You need everything from insulated pants to glacier glasses. You need a headlamp with a spare bulb and an ice axe.

And you'd need about 50 other things. But we think you should start with the stuff that sounds the coolest—*glacier glasses* and an *ice axe.*

And oh yeah, you'll only get 1/3 of the oxygen that's available to you at sea level.

How does the human body react when it has so much less oxygen than usual? You can look it up, but it's not pretty.

But it can be described in one word: *weakness.*

.................................................................................

*Is mental fatigue a thing? Can we get a doctor's excuse for that?*

In the same way, you're going to face your own "Everest" climbs in life. You'll have moments of mental, spiritual, relational, psychological and physical weakness.

But here's the good news: God meets you right there with His grace. Paul wrote about it:

> But he said to me, "My grace is sufficient for you, for my power is made perfect in weakness." Therefore I will boast all the more gladly about my weaknesses, so that Christ's power may rest on me. That is why, for Christ's sake, I delight in weaknesses, in insults, in hardships, in persecutions, in difficulties. For when I am weak, then I am strong (2 Corinthians 12:9-10).

Paul's weaknesses pointed to God's sufficient grace. Where Paul wasn't good or strong enough, he learned to depend on a good God. THIS IS ONE OF THE GREATEST PROMISES GOD GIVES US: HIS POWER WILL SHINE THROUGH OUR WEAKNESSES.

WHAT DOES IT MEAN TO DEPEND ON GOD? DON'T WRITE CHURCHY WORDS—PUT IT IN YOUR OWN LANGUAGE.

..................................................................................

..................................................................................

IN WHAT AREAS DO YOU NEED GOD'S POWER TO SHINE THROUGH YOUR WEAKNESS?

..................................................................................

..................................................................................

..................................................................................

PRAY A PRAYER OF DEPENDENCE. SOMETHING LIKE, "GOD, YOU KNOW THE AREAS WHERE I'M WEAK. IN FACT, I JUST WROTE THEM DOWN. I INVITE YOU IN. SHOW OFF IN MY WEAKNESSES AND TEACH ME HOW TO LEAN ON YOU. THANK YOU THAT I CAN TRUST YOU EVEN WHEN I CAN'T TRUST MYSELF."

# DAY FOUR
## ESCAPE ARTIST

Why are prison escape attempts so fascinating? Maybe it's the *Mission: Impossible* storyline. Or maybe it's because they almost never work.

In 1970 Billy Hayes was a 22-year-old American who got busted trying to smuggle a small amount of drugs out of Turkey. (The country, not the bird. That would be *really* weird.) He was thrown into a remote island prison where he received a steady string of beatings and concluded that his life was probably over.

Six months later Hayes snuck out of the prison, stole a boat, and rowed 17 miles to the mainland. Hayes knew his blonde hair would attract attention, so he dyed it black. Barefoot, he then walked for miles and swam across a huge river to the Greek border. Eventually, Hayes made it safely back to the United States.[14] Again, *fascinating*. And maybe these escape stories fascinate us because they make us wonder what we would do in that situation. How would we get out?

Do you ever feel like temptation is your own personal prison? Maybe there's some type of sin in your life that makes you feel like you deserve to be in that prison. And every time it knocks at your door, you think, *There's no way I can escape this. I've already gone back to it so many times.*

Let's look at one of God's incredible promises, courtesy of Paul:

> *No temptation has overtaken you except what is common to mankind. And God is faithful; he will not let you be tempted beyond what you can bear. But when you are tempted, he will also provide a way out so that you can endure it (1 Corinthians 10:13).*

God promises to be with you. And when you're tempted, He promises to give you a way out, every time. Like we said yesterday, your weakness provides an opportunity for God to show off His power, if you allow Him.

WHY DO WE SOMETIMES GIVE IN TO TEMPTATION EVEN THOUGH. . .

WE KNOW WE SHOULDN'T?

WE KNOW WE'LL FEEL GUILTY AFTERWARDS?

......................................................................................................

......................................................................................................

......................................................................................................

NAME SOME POSITIVE THINGS YOU CAN DO WHEN YOU FEEL TEMPTED.

......................................................................................................

......................................................................................................

......................................................................................................

SPEND A FEW MINUTES PRAYING. ASK GOD TO SHOW YOU HIS ESCAPE ROUTES THE NEXT TIME YOU FEEL TEMPTED.

# DAY FIVE

Juliane Koepcke was 17 years old when she and her mother flew to see her father in Pucallpa, Peru (try saying that one a few times fast). During their flight the plane was struck by lightning in a severe thunderstorm. The plane disintegrated. Now only strapped to her seat, Koepcke plummeted three miles back to earth. Yet somehow she miraculously survived that landing, suffering only a broken collarbone and a gash to her right arm.

She spent 10 days looking for help in the jungle. She survived mosquito infections, maggot infestations (don't ask) and a fun canoe ride through water teeming with crocodiles and piranhas.[15] We'd like to see Tom Cruise do that.

Koepcke cheated death. And we can't help but cheer for her. Because for most of us, death is at the top of our list of Things to Fear.

The good news for us is that Jesus didn't just cheat death. He **DEFEATED** it. Paul says it this way:

> For what I received I passed on to you as of first importance: that Christ died for our sins according to the Scriptures, that he was buried, that he was raised on the third day according to the Scriptures
> (1 Corinthians 15:3-4).

Later he adds,

> *"Where, O death, is your victory?Where, O death, is your sting?" The sting of death is sin, and the power of sin is the law. But thanks be to God! He gives us the victory through our Lord Jesus Christ (1 Corinthians 15:55-56).*

Jesus Christ overcame death. No one, except Jesus, has come back from the dead to tell us what's on the other side—**LIFE**. We can trust that this life is not the end.

Jesus overcame sin and death. That's why you and I can have what Paul calls "victory." We can have hope that goes beyond right now. We can have strength when we face temptation and weakness. We can have courage. We can trust God, even when we encounter rejection, loneliness and fear.

WHAT ARE SOME OF YOUR GREATEST FEARS RIGHT NOW?

........................................................................................

........................................................................................

........................................................................................

WHAT WOULD IT LOOK LIKE FOR YOU TO LIVE FREE INSTEAD OF BEING CONTROLLED BY THOSE FEARS?

........................................................................................

........................................................................................

........................................................................................

NAME SOME OF GOD'S PROMISES THAT ARE FOR YOU RIGHT NOW.

........................................................................................................

........................................................................................................

........................................................................................................

WHICHEVER PROMISES YOU LISTED (EVEN IF YOU ONLY LISTED ONE), TAKE SOME TIME AND THANK GOD FOR THEM. THEN, TYPE THOSE PROMISES IN A NOTE ON YOUR PHONE SO YOU CAN SEE THEM THROUGHOUT THE DAY TOMORROW.

# WEEK THREE: WHAT'S MY PURPOSE?

**How often are you asked this question: "What do you want to do with your life?"** No big deal, right? Someone is just wondering what your plan is for the *next few decades*. Meanwhile you're not even sure what you're doing for lunch. (We vote Taco Bell).

The person asking this question is usually a parent, grandparent, teacher, or school advisor. Though they mean well, it's probably frustrating to think of an answer. Why? Because while everyone wants you to have a plan, no one seems to have a plan for how you can *make* a plan. In other words, how do you even begin to figure out your next step in life? HOW CAN YOU DISCOVER WHAT GOD HAS DESIGNED YOU TO DO?

The Apostle Paul figured it out eventually. Maybe it's because he recognized his own unique skills and talents, like writing, public speaking, and shipwreck survival (see Week 1). But it's more likely that Paul uncovered his purpose as he experienced some defining moments. These were events in his story that changed the direction of his life. They were points on his timeline where he could clearly see a **BEFORE** and **AFTER**.

All of the best stories contain these kinds of moments. Every book you've read, every show you've watched, and every movie you've seen contains at least one defining moment—an event that redirects someone's entire story.

When Katniss Everdeen takes her sister's place in *The Hunger Games*, it's a choice that not only impacts her life, but the future of humanity *(no pressure)*. When Elsa accidentally freezes her sister at the beginning of *Frozen*, it's a moment that changes their lives and the future of their world. (See a trend here? And no, you can't pretend you don't love *Frozen*.)

Every one of us has defining moments in our lives. And while humanity's future probably isn't on the line, the stakes can still feel huge. Maybe it was when your family moved to a new state.

# HOW CAN YOU DISCOVER WHAT GOD HAS DESIGNED YOU TO DO?

Maybe it happened when that girl or that guy dumped you. Maybe it was the moment when your parents told you they were getting a divorce. Maybe it was the moment when you realized it was time start thinking about college and you still have no idea what to do. No matter the size of the moment, it changed your life in some way.

But these events can do something else. They can launch us into God's purpose and plan for our lives.

Exhibit A: The life of Paul. Paul had so many defining moments that it takes something really crazy to stand out. Something like this:

> Paul and his companions traveled throughout the region of Phrygia and Galatia, having been kept by the Holy Spirit from preaching the word in the province of Asia. When they came to the border of Mysia, they tried to enter Bithynia, but the Spirit of Jesus would not allow them to. So they passed by Mysia and went down to Troas.
>
> During the night Paul had a vision of a man of Macedonia standing and begging him, "Come over to Macedonia and help us." After Paul had seen the vision, we got ready at once to leave for Macedonia, concluding that God had called us to preach the gospel to them (Acts 16:6-10).

A vision. Of a person. In the middle of the night. This sounds more like a scary movie than a defining moment. But this event had a huge effect on what Paul did next.

Let's recap first: Paul miraculously met Jesus during an epic road trip, was blinded during this encounter, then had his eyesight restored a few days later. We're going to file that under **LIFE-CHANGING MOMENTS.**

And it definitely changed his life. Paul went from being a murderer to being a missionary. But believe it or not, that first encounter with Jesus only got him to the first stop on God's plan for his life. He was spreading the Gospel, but only to his fellow Jews. God wanted *everyone* to hear it.

Macedonia (or Macedon) was an area in the northern part of Greece. Paul had yet to show any real interest in heading that direction. But once he received this vision of a Greek man begging Paul to bring him the Gospel, the plan shifted. Notice what Paul does: *"We got ready AT ONCE to leave for Macedonia, concluding that God had called us to preach the gospel to them."* The Gospel wasn't just for the Jewish people. It was for the Greeks (and all the other non-Jews), too. But they had no one to tell them about it.

Paul would go on to plant numerous churches throughout Greece, which spread Christianity far beyond where it began. His letters to some of those churches make up part of the New Testament. In one letter to a church in Galatia, Paul shares how his encounter with Jesus changed the course of his life.

> *Dear brothers and sisters, I want you to understand that the gospel message I preach is not based on mere human reasoning. I received my message from no human source, and no one taught me. Instead, I received it by direct revelation from Jesus Christ.*
>
> *You know what I was like when I followed the Jewish religion—how I violently persecuted God's church. I did my best to destroy it. I was far ahead of my fellow Jews in my zeal for the traditions of my ancestors.*

*But even before I was born, God chose me and called
me by his marvelous grace. Then it pleased him to reveal
his Son to me so that I would proclaim the Good News
about Jesus to the Gentiles* [16]
*(Galatians 1:11-16b NLT).*

PAUL ENCOUNTERED JESUS, AND THEN PAUL DISCOVERED
PURPOSE.

His talents and abilities were the same as they had always been.
Before Paul encountered Jesus, he was talented and driven. After
he met Jesus, he was just as talented and driven. He was still
a natural leader. He just used those talents in a different way.
So what changed the course of his life? Paul found his purpose
in defining moments. These experiences didn't *change* Paul's
passion, talents, and drive.

They channeled them.

Over the next few days, we're going to spend some time looking
at what makes you, you. We're going to explore your talents
and strengths. And we're going to look back at some of your
defining moments. For some of you, these moments will clearly
stand out in your mind. And for others, your defining moments
are still down the road. Either way, we'll take a look at how these
moments can give your life focus, purpose and direction.

But no late-night visions. We promise.

# DAY ONE
## FOLLOW THE LEADER

Let's talk about some things you can do **WITHOUT** a guide, but probably shouldn't:

- African safari
- Whitewater rafting
- Parachuting out of a plane
- Deep-sea scuba diving
- Alcatraz prison tour

Why? For starters, just consider some of the things that a guide could help you *avoid* in these situations: an angry hippopotamus, surprise waterfalls, pulling out your chute and landing on a highway, becoming shark bait and the ghost of Al Capone.

But beyond that, think about what they could **SHOW** you that you might not have seen otherwise. Think about what they can **TEACH** you that you might not have known. Think about how much more you can **EXPERIENCE** with a guide.

Even though Paul was a take-charge type of guy, the story of the Macedonian man makes it clear that Paul responded to God's direction. In other words, Paul had a Guide. Look at these two excerpts from the story:

- *When they came to the border of Mysia, they tried to enter Bithynia, but the Spirit of Jesus would not allow them to (Acts 16:7).*

- *. . . We got ready at once to leave for Macedonia, concluding that God had called us to preach the gospel to them (Acts 16:10).*

Words like **NOT ALLOW** and **CALLED** emphasize the point: Paul was a leader who was willing to be led by God. But think about what Paul learned, witnessed and experienced because of it. Paul became a key part of changing the trajectory of Christianity forever!

You can be led, too. God is more than willing to be personally involved in the plan and purpose of your life. And friends, *that* is grace. The God of Paul wants to be the God of you! The Spirit that led Paul to Macedonia is the Spirit that will lead you.

You're smart. You have access to endless technology. You can figure things out faster than any generation before you. There is an answer to almost any problem right at your fingertips. But YOU CAN AVOID SO MUCH BAD AND EXPERIENCE SO MUCH GOOD WHEN YOU ACKNOWLEDGE AND INVITE GOD INTO YOUR PLAN. And who better to lead you than the One who created you? The only One who knows you better than you know yourself?

DEFINE GUIDE. DESCRIBE WHAT A GUIDE DOES.

.............................................................................................................

.............................................................................................................

.............................................................................................................

USING THOSE SAME TERMS, WHAT WOULD IT LOOK LIKE FOR YOU TO ALLOW GOD TO GUIDE YOUR LIFE? (If you're not sure to start, think about these areas first and then add some of your own: dating, money, future plans.)

....................................................................................................................

....................................................................................................................

....................................................................................................................

WHAT HOLDS YOU BACK FROM INVITING GOD TO TAKE THE LEAD?

....................................................................................................................

....................................................................................................................

....................................................................................................................

SPEND A FEW MINUTES PRAYING. THANK GOD FOR CARING ABOUT THE DETAILS OF YOUR LIFE.

INVITE GOD TO GUIDE YOUR LIFE. MAYBE START WITH SOMETHING LIKE, "GOD, YOU KNOW ME BETTER THAN I KNOW ME. AND I BELIEVE YOU WANT A GOOD LIFE FOR ME. I INVITE YOU TO TAKE THE LEAD. SHOW ME WHICH DOORS I SHOULD WALK THROUGH AND WHICH DOORS I SHOULDN'T. HELP ME AVOID WHAT YOU WANT ME TO AVOID AND EXPERIENCE WHAT YOU WANT ME TO EXPERIENCE."

# DAY TWO
## BIG STEPS

On July 20, 1969, we put a man on the moon. We (meaning NASA) launched Neil Armstrong and Buzz Aldrin into space. These guys saw the moon up close and personal, and then they returned home safely. And it was the United States of America that made it happen.

The moon landing was a turning point for the U.S., space exploration, and mankind in general. Armstrong himself said it best: "That's one small step for man, one giant leap for mankind."

Needless to say, that was a big moment. Similarly, Christianity had its man-on-the-moon moment when Paul had the vision of the Macedonian man. Because of that, the Gospel began to spread westward. And through the efforts of Paul and a few others, Europe and the Western world eventually heard about Jesus.

Wow.

The cool thing is, your life consists of man-on-the-moon moments as well. Those moments may not revolutionize the future of Astronomy or Christianity (Or maybe they will. Why not?), but here's what we know for sure. Those moments are important. And they are personal to **YOU**.

THINK ABOUT A FEW OF THOSE MOMENTS RIGHT NOW— SITUATIONS OR EVENTS THAT CHANGED EVERYTHING FOR YOU. WHAT ARE THEY? WHEN DID THEY HAPPEN? GOT SOME LIFE-DEFINING MOMENTS IN MIND? GOOD.

Let's start with the not-so-fun stuff. WRITE DOWN A *NEGATIVE* DEFINING MOMENT OR TWO IN YOUR LIFE:

..................................................................................................

..................................................................................................

..................................................................................................

SPEND A FEW MINUTES PRAYING. ASK GOD TO COMFORT YOU AS YOU REMEMBER THOSE MOMENTS. THEN, ASK HIM TO LEVERAGE THOSE MOMENTS TO PREPARE YOU TO HELP OTHER PEOPLE WHO ARE GOING THROUGH SIMILAR THINGS.

NOW, WRITE DOWN A *POSITIVE* DEFINING MOMENT OR TWO IN YOUR LIFE. IT COULD BE AS SIMPLE AS A CONTEST YOU WON OR AN ENCOURAGING WORD SOMEONE SAID TO YOU.

..................................................................................................

..................................................................................................

..................................................................................................

SPEND A FEW MINUTES THANKING GOD FOR HIS GRACE IN THOSE MOMENTS. ASK HIM TO USE THOSE EVENTS TO HELP YOU DISCOVER MORE OF HIS PURPOSE FOR YOU.

# DAY THREE
## GOOD GENES

Will Smith is talented. No doubt about that. *Newsweek* once called him the most powerful actor in Hollywood.[17] As of 2014, he had been a leading man in 21 movies, 17 of which grossed more than $100 million. In total, his films have grossed around $6.6 billion dollars.

And he's had a successful music career. So...yeah, he's talented.

Apparently his kids have acquired some of his brilliance. His son Jaden has already starred in a hit movie. Plus, he rapped on a Justin Bieber song (so there's *that*). His daughter Willow had her own radio hit, "Whip My Hair." If you're feeling a little sleepy right now, by the way, you should just whip your hair back and forth (just don't injure yourself).

The bottom line? Will Smith's kids inherited some talent from their dad.

Now let's talk about your dad. Not your dad on Earth, but your Heavenly Father—the One who created you. Did you know that He's pretty talented? When you see a sunset, a waterfall, enormous mountains, huge ocean waves, or a starlit sky, know that God is the One who invented it. He's the Writer, Designer, Architect and Creator of it all.

He's ridiculously creative. And as His child, you've inherited some of His skills. But, like many students, you may be convinced that you got the short end of the stick when it comes to talent. That someone else got more. *He's* a better guitar player. *She's* a better actress. *He's* a better three-point shooter. *She's* better at math.

The problem with thinking this way is that it moves your attention away from celebrating what God has given **YOU**. It keeps you from focusing on how God has uniquely wired **YOU**. And ultimately, it keeps you from honoring God with your gifts and talents because you're not even aware of them. Paul, who recognized that everyone is different and unique, wrote this in Ephesians 2:10:

> *For we are God's handiwork, created in Christ Jesus to do good works, which God prepared in advance for us to do.*

You are God's handiwork! Out of His grace, God has made you, **YOU**. He wants you to honor Him with your life. To do that, He's equipped you with skills and abilities that turn attention toward Him. But your skills and abilities aren't going to be just like those of the people around you. Your talents will be as unique as you are.

NAME SOME THINGS YOU'RE GOOD AT.

.............................................................................

.............................................................................

.............................................................................

NAME SOME THINGS YOU LOVE TO DO.

.............................................................................

.............................................................................

.............................................................................

WHAT IS ONE WAY YOU THINK GOD COULD USE YOUR TALENTS TO HELP SOMEONE ELSE?

............................................................................................

............................................................................................

............................................................................................

............................................................................................

SPEND SOME TIME PRAYING. ASK GOD TO OPEN YOUR EYES TO THE GIFTS, TALENTS, SKILLS AND ABILITIES THAT HE HAS GIVEN YOU (MAYBE SOME THAT YOU'VE NEVER EVEN BEEN AWARE OF BEFORE). THANK GOD FOR THEM. ASK GOD TO USE THEM FOR HIS PURPOSE.

# DAY FOUR
## IMITATION GAME

Do you do a lot of cleaning around the house? We imagine that only a small percentage of you who would answer, "**YES!**" The rest of you would say, "Well...I *do* clean my room, sort of, when my stepmom reminds me 5 or 6 or 28 times." If that's the case, you've probably never heard of all-purpose cleaner. It's a spray bottle full of crazy chemicals that allow you to clean windows, appliances, kitchen surfaces and mop floors, using only one product.

But imagine if you found that item in a cabinet for the first time and had no context for cleaning products at all. You'd never seen any before. You might see "all-purpose cleaner" and think:

- Mouthwash. So I can clean my teeth with it (which would put you directly in the hospital, by the way. Don't do it.)*
- Dog shampoo. So I can groom Tator Tot, my border collie, with it.
- Engine flush. So I can clean out my car's engine with it.
- Software. So I can clean out my computer's hard drive with it.

All of those uses would be a bad idea, of course. Your computer would be fried and Tator Tot would be poisoned. Why? Because even though "all-purpose" implies you can use it for anything, the makers of that product had other "all purposes" in mind when they created it. Your best bet would be to turn the bottle around and read the instructions.

* *Seriously*

In the same way, God looks at you and says, "Because I created you, I have the best idea of what you should do. I know My intentions for you—what My plan is for your life. Don't just try to figure it out on your own. Look to Me, your Maker."

Paul gives us a starting point in Ephesians 5:1-2a:

> Imitate God, therefore, in everything you do, because you are his dear children. Live a life filled with love, following the example of Christ (NLT).[18]

Follow the example of Jesus. When God created you, He gave you those instructions. It doesn't mean you're going to be perfect like Jesus was. It means you observe, learn from and try to imitate what He was like. For example:

1. He had a compassionate heart.
2. He showed kindness and acceptance to people (even hard-to-love people).
3. He honored people in authority.
4. He forgave people who wronged Him.
5. He spent time with God.

The list could go on and on. But let's start simple.

WHICH ONE OF THESE 5 THINGS DO YOU MOST NEED TO WORK ON RIGHT NOW?

..........................................................................................................

..........................................................................................................

..........................................................................................................

ASK GOD TO SHOW YOU MORE OF WHAT IT MEANS TO LIVE LIKE JESUS IN THAT AREA.

One last thing: imagine...

*THE ORIGINAL "YOU" THAT GOD CREATED
*PLUS YOU, LIVING LIKE JESUS
*WHAT WOULD THAT EQUAL?

We don't know for sure. But we bet it would be pretty incredible!

# DAY FIVE
## LEARNING TO SHARE

On the road to Damascus, Saul encountered grace. Jesus graciously showed up, even when Saul didn't deserve the visit. That encounter changed everything. After that moment Saul went on to share that grace with everyone he could. He knew that this grace wasn't just for him.

Grace is **FOR** you. God loves you, accepts you, and forgives you—for free. End of story. It's a gift. You can't earn it. You simply receive it.

But grace should also flow **THROUGH** you to other people. Grace will still be grace, even if you do nothing with it. But when you have the opportunity to share it with people you know, why not go for it?

When it comes to God, church, Jesus, and the Bible, we usually hesitate to talk about any of it. We're afraid of embarrassing ourselves. We're worried that we won't know answers to tough questions. We're convinced that we'll be viewed as obnoxious or offensive.

But that's the wrong mindset. You're not giving knowledge, an opinion, or a lecture. You're giving grace. Think of it this way: you are giving others the **OPPORTUNITY** to encounter the matchless, amazing grace of Jesus Christ! When you share grace, you give people a chance to realize something that very few people ever realize:

THEY ARE LOVED AND ACCEPTED. FOR FREE.

When you develop a heart that is passionate about God's grace, it will cause you to get excited when you talk about your faith. This doesn't mean you'll start preaching on street corners. It just means that you'll enjoy your relationship with God. And when the right opportunities come up, you'll want to share that with others through your actions and your words.

The Gospel of Jesus offers hope. Are you offering hope to people? The Gospel of Jesus accepts people. Are you accepting people? The Gospel of Jesus is all about serving people. Are you serving people? The end goal of the Gospel is for people to know Jesus and His grace.

Paul learned this through a vision, a dream of a man from Macedonia begging to hear about Jesus.

WHO IS YOUR "MACEDONIAN MAN"? IN OTHER WORDS, WHO IS SOMEONE WHO COULD BENEFIT FROM THE OPPORTUNITY OF ENCOUNTERING GOD'S GRACE? SOMEONE WHO WOULD BENEFIT FROM BEING ACCEPTED, SERVED OR LOVED?

..............................................................................................................

..............................................................................................................

..............................................................................................................

PRAY THAT GOD WILL SEND SOMEONE INTO THAT PERSON'S LIFE WHO WILL SHOW THEM GRACE AND TELL GOD YOU'RE WILLING TO BE THAT PERSON.

WHAT WOULD IT LOOK LIKE FOR YOU TO ENJOY YOUR RELATIONSHIP WITH GOD MORE? WHAT WOULD YOU DO DIFFERENTLY? HOW WOULD YOU THINK DIFFERENTLY?

..................................................................................

..................................................................................

..................................................................................

HOW IS "ENJOYING YOUR RELATIONSHIP WITH GOD" CONNECTED TO WHAT OTHERS THINK ABOUT GOD?

..................................................................................

..................................................................................

..................................................................................

PRAY THAT GOD WILL GIVE YOU THE COURAGE TO LIVE LIKE PAUL, BRINGING THE GOOD NEWS OF GRACE TO THOSE AROUND YOU. ASK HIM TO USE YOU TO OFFER PEOPLE HOPE AND ACCEPTANCE. PRAY FOR OPPORTUNITIES TO SERVE PEOPLE, AND PRAY FOR THE COURAGE TO ACT WHEN THE OPPORTUNITY ARISES.

# WEEK FOUR: WHAT'S MY COM- MUNITY?

**What does the perfect Christian look like to you?** Do you think of a person who smiles a lot? (Their teeth are celebrity-level white, of course.) Do they carry themselves a certain way? Do they seem calm? Nice? Does she only wear dresses? Does he only wear khakis and a button-down?

In most people's minds, the perfect Christian walks, talks and acts...well, *perfectly*. They *used* to struggle with sin, but now they've moved beyond that. They *used* to have more issues than a magazine, but now have zero problems in life. They *used* to listen to the radio, but now they only have worship playlists on their Spotify account.

If a person works hard enough and overcomes their issues, they eventually become elite Christians, right? They're like role models for the rest of us. They volunteer at church and help others with their problems. They're needed, but never needy. They graduate into "Super Christians"—people who rise above everyone else.

Of course, not all of us can live like that. But it does feel like we're all on some kind of cosmic ladder or holy ranking system, and some rank higher on that ladder than others.

PAUL DIDN'T SEE IT THAT WAY.

Considering that Paul wrote so much of the New Testament, you would think he'd consider himself an elite Christian—way better than any newbie and probably most veterans, too. But as Paul grew in his faith, he didn't try to stand apart. Instead he got more involved with other people.

Back when Paul was Saul, we first hear about him as he's charging toward Damascus with his anonymous entourage of thugs. We don't find any details in Scripture about this group. They're all just rolling together as one committed crew, bound together by purpose, but not necessarily friendship.

But check out this passage from the book of Acts. Here we see a picture of Paul much later in his life. He's rolling with a different group of people now.

> When the uproar was over, Paul sent for the believers and encouraged them. Then he said good-bye and left for Macedonia. While there, he encouraged the believers in all the towns he passed through. Then he traveled down to Greece, where he stayed for three months. He was preparing to sail back to Syria when he discovered a plot by some Jews against his life, so he decided to return through Macedonia.
>
> Several men were traveling with him. They were Sopater son of Pyrrhus from Berea; Aristarchus and Secundus from Thessalonica; Gaius from Derbe; Timothy; and Tychicus and Trophimus from the province of Asia.[19] (Acts 20:1-4 NLT).

We get it. When we see a list of names like this in the Bible, our eyes glaze over and we think, "Maybe I should check my phone." Or, "A taco sounds delicious right now." (I mean, it does.) But while these lists can seem irrelevant, the names in this verse aren't just random people. They were intentionally included, and they offer us some insight into Paul's life at that moment.

No longer was he a lone-ranger zealot, surrounded by nameless goons. Now he was a part of something where the relationships were just as important as the mission. Sopater, Secundus, and Trophimus weren't just guys who really needed nicknames. They were people who mattered enough to be included in Paul's story.

BECAUSE AS PAUL GREW IN GRACE, HE ALSO GREW IN COMMUNITY.

And he grew along side a very diverse group. When **SAUL** was traveling to Damascus, his entourage was filled with guys just like him—men who thought the same, dressed the same and looked the same. Years later **PAUL** traveled back to Damascus with a different group. This time, his friends resembled the United Nations. Three guys were from Northern Greece, two were from near Galatia, and two were from a city near Ephesus. Paul was no longer surrounded by a bunch of identical "Yes" men. Each friend brought his own specific background, culture and worldview to the group.

Paul's vision of community was also closely linked with the local church. Later in this same passage from Acts, Paul meets with the elders from a church he planted in Ephesus.

*"And now, compelled by the Spirit, I am going to Jerusalem, not knowing what will happen to me there. I only know that in every city the Holy Spirit warns me that prison and hardships are facing me.*

*I have not coveted anyone's silver or gold or clothing. You yourselves know that these hands of mine have supplied my own needs and the needs of my companions. In everything I did, I showed you that by this kind of hard work we must help the weak, remembering the words the Lord Jesus himself said: 'It is more blessed to give than to receive.'"*

*When Paul had finished speaking, he knelt down with all of them and prayed. They all wept as they embraced him and kissed him. What grieved them most was his statement that they would never see his face again. Then they accompanied him to the ship*
*(Acts 20:22-23 and 33-38).*

The end of this passage shows how much Paul loved his community. It shares a moment where his friends from the church are crying over him and praying for him. It's a powerful scene of real friendship.

Paul is one of the most famous Christians in history. His words and insights have impacted every believer after him. But no matter how great Paul grew in his accomplishments and reputation, he never outgrew the need for other people. He understood that NO MATTER WHERE WE ARE IN OUR JOURNEY WITH GOD, WE NEED PEOPLE EVERY STEP OF THE WAY.

In the book of Romans, Paul directly encourages believers to pursue meaningful relationships.

> For by the grace given me I say to every one of you: Do not think of yourself more highly than you ought, but rather think of yourself with sober judgment, in accordance with the faith God has distributed to each of you. For just as each of us has one body with many members, and these members do not all have the same function, so in Christ we, though many, form one body, and each member belongs to all the others. We have different gifts, according to the grace given to each of us... (Romans 12:3-6)

Paul was sharing an important truth: As we grow in our relationship with God, we should also grow in love, relationships, and service. Paul often linked grace and community. In other words, Paul was saying, "Because of the grace we've been given, let's show each other grace."

So what does this look like? We give the people around us a break. We don't expect perfection from others, and we don't talk badly about them when they fail. We get more involved with our church and actually help out by volunteering. We surround ourselves with people who can walk with us through life, instead of pretending that we can handle it all on our own. We show people grace and kindness, not judgment and selfishness.

As we grow in grace, we grow in community.

NO MATTER
WHERE WE
ARE IN OUR
JOURNEY WITH
GOD, WE NEED
PEOPLE EVERY
STEP OF THE
WAY.

# DAY ONE
## MIX-UP

There are some unique people in the world. We're unique in how we look, how we talk and how we interact with others. We also value different things. Take Charlotte Lee, for example. Charlotte, a 32-year-old from Seattle, has acquired more than 5,000 rubber ducks that she stores (hides?) in her basement.[20] Then there's Jian Yang, a gentleman who collects Barbies. He's got more than 6,000 dolls and has spent almost $400,000 on his hobby.[21] Becky Martz, on the other hand, has amassed over 8,000 stickers from bananas she bought at the grocery store.[22]

People like different things (some of those things are stranger than others). But you don't have to do a Google search to find people different than you. Look at the girl sitting beside you in geometry or the guy across the aisle from you in band. Every day we encounter people with different stories. Different backgrounds. Different differences. And these differences can be good things, right? They add variety. They make things interesting.

But they can also make things more complicated.

A guy may get some questioning looks for blaring country music when he pulls into the parking lot at school. A girl from a conservative religious background might get laughed at for how she dresses. A guy with an accent may get teased (or, in some cases, get more dates).

WHEN YOU THINK OF SOMEONE WHO IS "DIFFERENT" FROM YOU, WHO IS THE FIRST PERSON THAT COMES TO MIND?

........................................................................................................

........................................................................................................

........................................................................................................

When human beings interact with each other in community, regardless of how loose or close-knit that community might be, we act like…well, humans. We're imperfect. We screw up. We hurt each other. We use our differences as a way to measure ourselves against others. Sometimes we act like we're better because we're different. Or maybe we're considered less-than because we're different.

The truth is, living in community with people who are different than us can be difficult. It requires us to be a little uncomfortable. It requires us to overlook things that offend us. It requires **GRACE** (*for* us and *from* us). But without community, life just isn't as much fun. It's not as rich. It's not as purpose-filled. And ultimately, it's not what God designed for us.

God designed us to live in community.

Have you ever been in a stadium where the home team won? Maybe it was a close game or match, and in those last few seconds, the tension in the room was tangible? When the buzzer to end the game sounded, what happened? The crowd went wild, right? The energy released in that moment was immeasurable. It was electric. You got caught up in it—and you may not have even cared who won or lost.

Now imagine that same game with one person in the stadium. Not quite the same effect, right? That's because so many things in life are better when they're done together. When life is lived in community, it's richer. It's deeper. The energy changes. It *moves* you.

Living in community is not easy, but it's worth it.

THINK ABOUT SOMEONE YOU'RE CLOSE TO—A TEAMMATE, A FRIEND, SOMEONE IN YOUR SMALL GROUP.

WHAT'S A DIFFERENCE BETWEEN YOU THAT MAKES YOU UNCOMFORTABLE OR THAT ANNOYS YOU?

..............................................................................................

..............................................................................................

..............................................................................................

WHAT IS ONE WAY YOU CAN SHOW GRACE TO THAT PERSON?

..............................................................................................

..............................................................................................

..............................................................................................

SPEND A FEW MINUTES PRAYING. TELL GOD YOU WANT TO LIVE YOUR LIFE LIKE HE DESIGNED—IN COMMUNITY. ASK HIM TO HELP YOU UNDERSTAND WHAT THAT TRULY MEANS.

# DAY TWO
## BAD REPUTATION

If you type "Christians are" into Google, here are some of the auto-filled search terms you'll immediately see:

Christians are <u>annoying</u>.
Christians are <u>crazy</u>.
Christians are <u>liars</u>.

Christianity has a reputation, doesn't it?

Now, if you type, "Jesus is" into Google, here are the results:

Jesus is <u>risen</u>.
Jesus is <u>alive</u>.
Jesus is <u>love</u>.

WHY DO YOU THINK JESUS FOLLOWERS HAVE A DIFFERENT REPUTATION THAN JESUS?

........................................................................................

........................................................................................

........................................................................................

Chances are your answer had something to do with the way Christians treat people. The way we treat someone doesn't just affect how others view *us*, it also creates a general reputation for others *like* us. But Christians don't just have a reputation for treating non-believers poorly. We also have been known to gossip, argue, and attack those inside the Church as well.

Maybe that's why, in Philippians 2:1-2, Paul tells us:

> Is there any encouragement from belonging to Christ? Any fellowship together in the spirit? Are your hearts tender and compassionate? Then make me truly happy by agreeing wholeheartedly with each other, loving one another, and working together with one mind and purpose [23] (NLT).

The Message version puts Paul's words to the church in Philippi this way:

> If you've gotten anything at all out of following Christ, if his love has made any difference in your life, if being in a community of the Spirit means anything to you, if you have a heart, if you care— then do me a favor: Agree with each other, love each other, be deep-spirited friends...Don't be obsessed with getting your own advantage. Forget yourselves long enough to lend a helping hand. [24]

Basically, changing the way others think of Christianity can begin with changing the way we treat other Christians.

IS THERE ANYONE IN YOUR STUDENT MINISTRY YOU NEED TO ASK FORGIVENESS FROM?

.................................................................................................

.................................................................................................

.................................................................................................

IS THERE ANYONE IN YOUR STUDENT MINISTRY YOU NEED
TO FORGIVE?

...............................................................................................

...............................................................................................

...............................................................................................

If a non-believer looks at our relationships with other believers, they should see "deep-spirited friends" who show each other grace. If what they see is bickering, pettiness, gossip and betrayal, why would they ever want to be a Christ-follower? Their issue clearly isn't with Christ—it's with us.

SPEND A FEW MINUTES PRAYING. ASK GOD TO HELP YOU FORGET YOURSELF AND EXTEND GRACE TO SOMEONE INSIDE YOUR CHURCH OR STUDENT MINISTRY. ASK HIM TO SHOW YOU WHAT PART YOU CAN PLAY IN BRINGING UNITY TO THE GROUP.

# DAY THREE

## SELFIE

How many times during a day do you look in the mirror? (Or in the front-facing camera lens of your cell phone?) After you wake up, sure. Getting dressed, of course. Maybe you glance at your makeup and/or teeth before walking into school. Throughout the day you might check yourself out after using the bathroom once or twice. Finally you probably stare bleary-eyed at your tired face as you brush your teeth before bed.

Today.com says that the average person looks in the mirror about 8 times a day.[25] That sounds about right, doesn't it? But think about this: if you held a mirror up to your face every time you thought about yourself, how many times would that add up to? It might just be easier to superglue a mirror to your hand!

WHAT DO YOUR THOUGHTS ABOUT YOURSELF TYPICALLY CENTER AROUND? YOUR FAMILY? WORK? SCHOOL? FRIENDS? THE OPPOSITE SEX?

.......................................................................................................

.......................................................................................................

Look, everybody thinks about themselves—this isn't a guilt trip. But there does come a point when the number of thoughts you have about yourself can outweigh the number of thoughts you have about anyone and *anything* else. And that's not a healthy (or a happy) place to be.

Think about it this way. When you hold a flashlight in the dark, which direction do you point the beam? Outward, right? That's how a flashlight was designed to be used. But what would happen if you held the beam of light directly at your own face? It would blind you. You wouldn't be able to see a thing. The device wouldn't help you as it was designed to do. In the same way, our lives become difficult and don't function properly when all of our prayers, thoughts and actions center on ourselves.

In his letter to the church at Philippi, Paul touched on this subject.

*Don't be selfish; don't try to impress others. Be humble, thinking of others as better than yourselves. Don't look out only for your own interests, but take an interest in others, too* [26] *(Philippians 2:3-4, NLT).*

Paul is saying, "Hey—take care of yourself. But don't *only* take care of yourself. Your life was meant to be lived with others in mind."

Then Paul adds the icing on the cake: *You must have the same attitude that Christ Jesus had* [27] *(Philippians 2:5 NLT).*

In this passage, Paul goes on to talk about how Jesus could have shined light only on Himself. Of all people, He had the right. But instead He chose the route of humility. He extended grace to us when we didn't deserve it. He used His time here to help us instead of focusing on Himself. And we need to reflect that kind of light to others.

The good news is, you can start with a small step today.
- Celebrate someone publicly.
- Pray for someone privately.
- Serve someone in secret.
- Ask someone questions and really listen to their answers.
- Give someone something without expecting anything in return.

WHAT'S ONE WAY YOU CAN SHINE LIGHT ON SOMEONE ELSE?

.........................................................................................

.........................................................................................

.........................................................................................

SPEND SOME TIME ASKING GOD TO HELP YOU BECOME MORE OTHERS-FOCUSED. COMMIT TO THE ONE THING YOU WROTE DOWN IN THE SPACE ABOVE.

# DAY FOUR
## CONFLICTED

Have you ever been pranked? Or are you typically the prankster? There is a certain scale to pranks, isn't there? There are fairly innocent ones like loosening the lid on a saltshaker right before someone uses it. And then there are bigger ones like...well, we don't want to give you any ideas.

But the fun (and dangerous) thing about pranks is that they usually escalate. Someone leaves a rubber snake in your bag. You give them a plate of cookies with toothpaste between them instead of icing. They come back at you with letting the air out of your tires. You one-up them by placing a "for sale" ad for their car online, complete with their phone number.*

Pranks tend to grow exponentially. And before long, you're not even sure who started it or why. Nobody wants to call a truce so the pranks keep going and going and going without an end in sight.

You know what else works like that? Conflict. It starts with a strange look. You don't like it so you ignore them in the lunchroom. In turn, they don't give you a ride after school. Then you block them on social media so they start a rumor about you. Eventually the two of you just end up hating each other, but you can't even remember how it all started.

And maybe you don't have an example this extreme, but you can probably think of at least one person you're annoyed with or angry

---

* Again, don't get any ideas.

with right now. That's because, when it comes to community, one thing is for sure:

YOU'RE GOING TO HAVE CONFLICT WITH OTHER PEOPLE.

You're going to get hurt by someone and you're going to hurt other people.

WHAT DO YOU TYPICALLY DO WHEN YOU'RE ANGRY WITH— OR HURT BY—SOMEONE?

.................................................................................................

.................................................................................................

.................................................................................................

The Bible actually has a lot to say about conflict. In Ephesians 4:31-32, Paul says:

> *Get rid of all bitterness, rage, anger, harsh words, and slander, as well as all types of evil behavior. Instead, be kind to each other, tenderhearted, forgiving one another, just as God through Christ has forgiven you* [28] *(NLT).*

Here's the thing about being kind: it's easy to be nice to people who are nice to you first. It's easy to forgive someone once they've apologized. But that's not what the Bible tells us to do. Paul is saying that we have to take the first step. He says to get rid of bitterness and forgive *"as God through Christ has forgiven you."* God created you before you could praise Him as Creator. God loved you before you could love Him back. God forgave you before you even knew you needed forgiving. God made the first move every time in His relationship with you.

As we allow God to restore and heal our relationship with Him, a natural response is for us to make the first move in restoring and healing relationships with others. In other words:

FORGIVE THEM THE WAY YOU WANT HIM TO FORGIVE YOU.

THINK ABOUT THE PERSON (OR PEOPLE) YOU ARE ANGRY WITH. WRITE DOWN WHAT YOU THINK THEY OWE YOU (EXAMPLES: RESPECT, A RETURN TEXT, AN APOLOGY, AN EXPLANATION, THE $10 YOU LENT THEM, ETC.)

..................................................................................................

..................................................................................................

NOW, THINK ABOUT YOURSELF. WHAT ARE SOME OF THE SINS AND OFFENSES AGAINST GOD THAT YOU'VE COMMITTED IN YOUR LIFE?

..................................................................................................

..................................................................................................

..................................................................................................

When you think of all you've been forgiven, it's impossible not to feel unworthy—unworthy of God's love, His mercy and His grace. One way you can say thank You to God is by forgiving others. This week, make the first move in any broken relationships that you have. Forgiveness doesn't happen overnight, but you can take the first step.

TAKE SOME TIME TO THANK GOD FOR HIS MERCY AND FORGIVENESS. ASK HIM TO SHOW YOU WHERE YOU NEED TO DEMONSTRATE GRACE AND OFFER FORGIVENESS.

# DAY FIVE
## CONTRAST

The early church grew rapidly because of two characteristics—its *generosity* and its *compassion*.

These Christ-followers were known for doing things that no one else would do. They interacted with and served the outcasts and lepers—those thought to be "unclean." They gave to the poor. They took care of widows and orphans. They went to war-torn villages and nursed survivors back to health. And they did it all without asking for anything in return.

*Compassion* and *generosity*—that was the reputation of the early church.

WHAT IS THE LOCAL CHURCH KNOWN FOR NOW? WHAT WORDS DO YOU THINK DESCRIBE THE REPUTATION OF THE CHURCHES (AND CHURCH PEOPLE) IN YOUR COMMUNITY?

In Philippians 2:14-16a, Paul advises the early Church:

*Do everything without grumbling or arguing, so that you may become blameless and pure, children of God without fault in a warped and crooked generation. Then you will shine among them like stars in the sky as you hold firmly to the word of life.*

Have you ever looked at the night sky without the distraction of city lights? Back in Paul's day, there was no electricity at all; just think about how black his dark sky was. When he says we should, "shine like stars," he means that, as believers, we should stand out. We should be distinct. We should be different from other people. But how?

*Do things without grumbling.*
*Do things without complaining.*

In other words, we need to get back to the world-altering attitudes of the early church. We must learn how to be compassionate and generous, but not just when it's easy. Not just when we get a T-shirt for it. Not just when we get school credit hours for it. Not just when it gets posted on Instagram.

We need to show compassion that defies logic. We need to show generosity that boggles the mind. And we need to do so quietly, diligently and cheerfully—without whining our way through it.

WE NEED TO BE SO RADICAL IN OUR LOVE FOR ALL PEOPLE THAT WE ARE LIKE STARS BURSTING INTO THE BLACKEST OF SKIES.

SPEND SOME TIME ASKING GOD HOW HE WANTS TO USE YOU. THEN, MAKE A LIST OF PLACES OR PEOPLE YOU CAN SERVE. IT MIGHT BE AT YOUR CHURCH, AT A NURSING HOME, OR MAYBE WITH SPECIAL NEEDS STUDENTS. WHERE CAN YOU BE *GENEROUS* AND *COMPASSIONATE*? PRAY THAT GOD WILL ENABLE YOUR CHURCH TO SHINE A LIGHT THAT MAKES IT STAND OUT IN A POSITIVE WAY.

# WEEK FIVE: HOW SHOULD I LIVE?

**So we (Ben and Jared) are student pastors.** And whenever we talk to a student about grace, the conversations often looks like this:

> STUDENT: So grace means I'm completely forgiven and God and I are cool, even if I don't deserve it?
>
> US: That's right.
>
> STUDENT: And I'm not just forgiven for what happened in the past, but what I do in the future too, right?
>
> US: Uh…yes.
>
> STUDENT: So basically grace means I can do whatever I want?
>
> US: (Face in hands. Considers a job change.)

We're not saying that every conversation on grace sounds like this. But inevitably, this question will come up: "If God forgives me for anything and everything, can I do whatever I want?"

This is a complicated question. On one hand, if we start drawing lines about what rules we need to follow for grace to "count," it's not grace anymore.

On the other extreme, if we can do any and every thing we want, our lives would lose all meaning. In other words, if Jesus simply offered us a lifetime hall pass and said, "Go sin like crazy," we'd be so messed up that we couldn't accomplish much good in the world.

The tension between grace and our behavior is not new. In fact, Paul addressed this very issue in his letter to the Roman church:

*Well then, should we keep on sinning so that God
can show us more and more of his wonderful grace?
Of course not! Since we have died to sin, how can we
continue to live in it? (Romans 6:1-2 NLT)*

To Paul, grace and behavior weren't enemies like Batman and
The Joker. They could actually get along all the time. The fact that
we're shown grace should directly impact our behavior. God's
grace is so amazing and so life changing that it shapes how we
think and act.

Let's take another look at Paul, later in his life. Paul was a prisoner
in Rome, waiting for his trial before Caesar. His crime? Telling
people about Jesus and grace.

Since sharing the Gospel in America doesn't result in a mug shot,
this sounds like a weird reason to go to jail. But back then, it was
common. If any of us were in that situation, we could probably
justify moping around, devising an escape plan or plotting
revenge against the Roman authorities.

Instead, Paul blows up our expectations of how we think someone
would respond to injustice.

*Three days after Paul's arrival, he called together the
local Jewish leaders. He said to them, "Brothers, I was
arrested in Jerusalem and handed over to the Roman
government, even though I had done nothing against
our people or the customs of our ancestors. The
Romans tried me and wanted to release me, because
they found no cause for the death sentence. But when
the Jewish leaders protested the decision, I felt it
necessary to appeal to Caesar, even though I had no
desire to press charges against my own people. I asked
you to come here today so we could get acquainted and
so I could explain to you that I am bound with this chain*

*because I believe that the hope of Israel—the Messiah—
has already come."*

*They replied, "We have had no letters from Judea
or reports against you from anyone who has come
here. But we want to hear what you believe, for the
only thing we know about this movement is that it is
denounced everywhere."*

*So a time was set, and on that day a large number of
people came to Paul's lodging. He explained and testified
about the Kingdom of God and tried to persuade them
about Jesus from the Scriptures. Using the Law of Moses
and the books of the prophets, he spoke to them from
morning until evening. Some were persuaded by the
things he said, but others did not believe.*

*For the next two years, Paul lived in Rome at his own
expense. He welcomed all who visited him, boldly
proclaiming the Kingdom of God and teaching about
the Lord Jesus Christ. And no one tried to stop him* [30]
*(Acts 28:17-24 and 30-31 NLT).*

Once Paul fully grasped what it meant to be forgiven—to live a
free life—he wanted to give that life back to God. Even while he
sat in prison. He didn't serve God because he thought he could
pay Jesus back or gain God's favor. Because of grace, he already
had God's favor. And that realization inspired Paul to fully commit
his life to God.

GRACE INSPIRED GRATITUDE.

In a letter to his close friend Timothy, near his death, Paul sums up
his life and ministry in a few powerful sentences:

GRACE
INSPIRED
GRATITUDE.

*As for me, my life has already been poured out as an offering to God. The time of my death is near. I have fought the good fight, I have finished the race, and I have remained faithful. And now the prize awaits me—the crown of righteousness, which the Lord, the righteous Judge, will give me on the day of his return. And the prize is not just for me but for all who eagerly look forward to his appearing* [31] *(2 Timothy 4:6-8 NLT).*

Paul knew God was pleased with him, and, in response, he gave his life back to God. What you do in your life matters. Your behavior, your direction, your impact—they all matter. But what you do doesn't affect whether God is okay with you. If you are in Christ, God has already declared you righteous. You've received His grace for everything you do.

We love the last line in this verse: *"And the prize is not just for me but for all who eagerly look forward to his appearing."* In other words, God's grace wasn't given to Paul because he was special or better than anyone else. It's for everyone.

And that means it's for you.

Paul is talking to Christians in the first century, and he's talking to us now. This gift—this grace—is for you. And just like Paul, you too can impact the world around you for Jesus. You can spend your life telling as many people as you possibly can about the amazing grace of a loving God who has forgiven even the worst of our sins. That is a life well lived. That is fighting the good fight and finishing the race.

Accept His grace. And then respond with gratitude.

# DAY ONE
## WALKING
## CONTRADICTION

......................................................................

W.H. Auden was a poet considered by many to be one of the greatest writers of the 20th century. He once made a comment that connects to what we're talking about this week:

> "I like committing crimes. God likes forgiving them. Really the world is admirably arranged.[32]"

That's the issue we all face when we truly encounter and accept God's grace. And it forces us to ask the question that Paul mentioned in Romans: *"Shall we go on sinning so that grace may increase?"*

Well, shall we?

As a potential answer to that question, let's look at something Paul says later in the book of Romans:

> *Therefore, I urge you, brothers and sisters, in view of God's mercy, to offer your bodies as a living sacrifice, holy and pleasing to God—this is your true and proper worship (Romans 12:1).*

Paul "urges" his readers, but the urge had a qualifier: "**IN VIEW OF GOD'S MERCY.**" In other words, Paul is saying, "Think about what God has done for you. *Respond to that.*"

DON'T THINK ABOUT WHAT YOU CAN GET AWAY WITH.

> *THINK ABOUT HOW GOD HAS DELIVERED YOU FROM YOUR SIN.*

DON'T TRY TO POSITION YOURSELF TO DO WHATEVER YOU WANT.

> *POSITION YOURSELF TO REMEMBER HOW GOD HAS SAVED YOU FROM THE PUNISHMENT YOU DESERVE.*

DON'T PAVE THE WAY FOR MORE SELFISHNESS AND DESTRUCTIVE BEHAVIOR.

> *REMEMBER HOW MERCY HAS PAVED THE WAY FOR GRACE, AND HOW GRACE HAS GIVEN YOU BLESSINGS THAT YOU DIDN'T EARN.*

Instead of offering yourself to sin, offer yourself to God as a living sacrifice. Say, "God, because of what You've done, I'm Yours. I'm all in. You're in charge."

DEFINE MERCY IN YOUR OWN WORDS.

.........................................................................................

.........................................................................................

.........................................................................................

LIST SPECIFIC WAYS THAT GOD HAS BEEN MERCIFUL TO YOU.

.........................................................................................

.........................................................................................

.........................................................................................

Here's a tough one (but we *are* at week five...questions should get tougher, right?): HOW WOULD YOUR LIFE LOOK DIFFERENT IF YOU OFFERED YOURSELF AS A "LIVING SACRIFICE" TO GOD IN RESPONSE TO HIS MERCY?

..........................................................................................

..........................................................................................

..........................................................................................

THANK GOD FOR HIS MERCY IN YOUR LIFE. ASK HIM TO TAKE THE LEAD. INVITE HIM INTO YOUR DECISIONS AND BEHAVIOR. THEN, THANK HIM FOR HIS MERCY AGAIN.

# DAY TWO
## CULTURE SHOCK

In 2015 a Kenyan marathon runner named Hyvon Ngetich collapsed two-tenths of a mile away from the finish line. She was in the lead at the time.

Race officials offered her a wheelchair, but she refused to use it. She literally crawled her way to the finish line. Amazingly, she still finished in third place. In fact, the race director was so impressed that he upgraded her award to second-place prize money.[33] How would you like to be the girl who finished fourth? "So you *didn't* beat the lady who was crawling?"

Ngetich was fine after they raised her blood sugar level back to normal. Let's be clear: we don't suggest finishing a race after you collapse—your body is sending you a pretty clear message at that point. But the simple reason why Ngetich finished the race is this: she chose to. She made a decision to keep moving.

The mind is a powerful thing.

In day one of this week, we looked at a verse where Paul urges us to offer our bodies as "living sacrifices" to God. In the next verse, Paul talks about how we live that out day by day. And it starts in our brain.

*Do not conform to the pattern of this world, but be transformed by the renewing of your mind. Then you will be able to test and approve what God's will is—his good, pleasing and perfect will (Romans 12:2).*

Culture is constantly trying to influence how we live. Every image, every magazine article, every commercial, every show, every marketing campaign is trying to convince us to think and act a certain way. Paul is telling us to be different. He's asking us to make a decision to let God be the commanding officer in our lives.

How? By re-programming our minds.

And here's the payoff: we will be in touch with God's "good, pleasing, and perfect will." In other words, we will be in direct contact with things that are pleasing to God.

Take a time out and think about this: God wants an amazing life for you. He wants more than a life where you just do right and don't mess up. He cares infinitely more about you living a life full of peace, joy, healthy relationships and satisfaction than He does about catching you doing something wrong. He has good and perfect gifts waiting for you.

IF YOU WENT ALONG WITH WHAT CULTURE WANTS FOR YOU, WHAT WOULD YOUR LIFE LOOK LIKE?

......................................................................................................

......................................................................................................

WHAT ARE SOME GOOD THINGS THAT YOU THINK GOD WANTS YOU TO EMBRACE?

......................................................................................................

......................................................................................................

NAME ONE AREA WHERE YOU NEED TO RE-PROGRAM YOUR MIND TO FOCUS ON THOSE GOOD THINGS?

...........................................................................................

...........................................................................................

SPEND SOME TIME PRAYING. INVITE GOD INTO YOUR THINKING. MAYBE PRAY SOMETHING LIKE, "GOD, YOU KNOW WHAT THE WORLD PULLS ME TOWARD. I CHOOSE YOU INSTEAD. HELP ME TO SEE THAT, OUT OF YOUR GRACE, YOU WANT GOOD THINGS FOR ME. LORD, PLEASE RE-PROGRAM MY MIND."

# DAY THREE
## ALL IN

.................................................................................................................

Do you love inspirational quotes?

No?

Hmmm. Well, that's too bad. We're going to throw some great ones at you anyway.

> *"We have to do the best we can. This is our sacred human responsibility."* – Albert Einstein

> *"I do the very best I know, the very best I can, and I mean to keep on doing so until the end."* – Abraham Lincoln

> *"No effort that we take to attain something beautiful is ever lost."* – Helen Keller

Near the end of his life, Paul wrote a letter to his young friend named Timothy. In very simple, yet epic, terms, Paul dropped an inspirational quote of his own:

> *I have fought the good fight, I have finished the race, I have kept the faith (2 Timothy 4:7).*

Paul was a part of something noble—sharing the Gospel with others. It was a good fight to be a part of, and Paul had given it his all. Does that mean he was perfect? Nope. Does that mean he always did the right thing? No. In fact, Paul openly admitted that he sometimes didn't do what was right, even when he wanted to.

But Paul was all in. What God wanted was more important than what Paul wanted. Whatever God asked Paul to do, he would obey, regardless of the cost to himself. And when he messed up, Paul turned to God for grace, forgiveness and restoration.

So what about you? What story would you tell about *your* life?

God's inviting you to go all-in, to commit your life to Him and let Him lead you.

WHAT WOULD YOUR LIFE LOOK LIKE IF YOU WENT ALL-IN WITH GOD? (We'll give you more space so you can go into detail.)

..............................................................................................

..............................................................................................

..............................................................................................

..............................................................................................

..............................................................................................

..............................................................................................

..............................................................................................

WHAT'S ONE THING THAT'S HOLDING YOU BACK FROM LIVING OUT WHAT YOU WROTE ABOVE?

..............................................................................................

..............................................................................................

ASK GOD TO GIVE YOU THE COURAGE TO GO ALL-IN. ASK HIM TO HELP YOU WHEN YOU MESS, TO QUICKLY TURN TO HIM FOR HIS GRACE, FORGIVENESS, AND RESTORATION.

# DAY FOUR
## OVERFLOW

Globalanimal.org shares a 2005 story published by the *San Francisco Chronicle* newspaper:

*A Female humpback whale had become entangled in a spider web of crab traps and lines. She was weighted down by hundreds of pounds of traps that caused her to struggle to stay afloat. The whale also had hundreds of yards of line rope wrapped around her body, tail, torso, and a line tugging in her mouth.*

*A fisherman spotted the whale just east of the Farallon Islands (beyond the Golden Gate bridge) and radioed an environmental group for help. Within a few hours, the rescue team arrived. They determined that the whale was so bad off that the only way to save her was to dive in and untangle her. The team worked for hours, carefully slashing through the labyrinth of lines with curved knives. Eventually, they freed her.*

*The divers say that once the female humpback was free to move, she swam in what seemed like joyous circles. The whale then came back to each diver, one at a time, and gave each a nudge, pushing her rescuers gently around as she was thanking them. Some divers said it was the most beautiful experience of their lives.*[34]

We personally doubt that we'd stick around for a "nudge" from a grateful whale. But we do know this: that's an amazing story. And it's a perfect illustration provided by one of the most powerful animals in the world: when you recognize something that's done for you that you cannot do for yourself, gratitude just *happens*.

Paul states this exact idea in a beautiful way:

*All this is for your benefit, so that the grace that is reaching more and more people may cause thanksgiving to overflow to the glory of God (2 Corinthians 4:15).*

GRACE CREATES GRATITUDE. Not the kind of gratitude where you politely say thank you to grandma when she gives you a pair of black socks for Christmas. No, it's the kind of gratitude that overflows everywhere you go. When grace inspires gratitude in you, you say things like, "Wow, God, I can't imagine where my life would be without Your grace in my life. It's all You. You're amazing."

God wants to do some amazing things in and through your life. Why? Because of His grace. You'll benefit. Others will benefit. And God will get the credit.

IF ALL OF YOUR ACTIONS WERE MOTIVATED BY YOUR GRATEFULNESS TO GOD, WHAT WOULD YOU *START* DOING? WHAT WOULD YOU *STOP* DOING?

.............................................................................................

.............................................................................................

.............................................................................................

HOW WOULD THOSE ACTIONS AFFECT THE PEOPLE
AROUND YOU?

......................................................................................................

......................................................................................................

......................................................................................................

HOW WOULD YOUR GRATITUDE CHANGE YOUR RELATIONSHIP
WITH GOD?

......................................................................................................

......................................................................................................

......................................................................................................

SPEND A FEW MINUTES PRAYING. THANK GOD FOR HIS
GRACE. PRAY THAT IT WILL OVERFLOW OUT OF YOU THROUGH
GRATITUDE. PRAY THAT GRATITUDE WILL BE A PART OF
YOUR LIFE, YOUR RELATIONSHIP WITH OTHERS, AND YOUR
RELATIONSHIP WITH HIM.

# DAY FIVE
## CLIFF HANGER

Have you ever seen a movie that doesn't have a conclusive ending? The credits roll and you're like, "Wait...that's it?"

The book of Acts, which tells the story of Paul's life, ends just like that. It's kind of like, "There you go, people. That's all you get."

Check out the abrupt ending here:

> *For two whole years Paul stayed there in his own rented house and welcomed all who came to see him. He proclaimed the kingdom of God and taught about the Lord Jesus Christ—with all boldness and without hindrance! (Acts 28:30-31)*

But then what? Does he stay locked up in his house? Does he die? Does he invent the Internet? Come on, people!

Many scholars believe that Luke, the writer of Acts, ended the book in this way to imply that the movement wasn't over. It was going to continue.

And here we are, thousands of years later, and you're reading a journal about it. So I guess Luke was right.

Nothing has stopped the church. Nothing has stopped the Gospel. Paul offered people grace. He explained grace to people. He invited people to accept grace. And if you are a follower of Jesus, you're up next. Paul has passed that job on to you.

Paul shared the Gospel "with all boldness and without hindrance." He didn't beat people up. In fact, he welcomed people into a house that wasn't even his! He built relationships. And he offered something irresistible.

We'll repeat something we said in the introduction to this week: like Paul, you too can impact the world around you for Jesus. You can spend your life telling as many people as you possibly can about the amazing grace of a loving God who has forgiven even the worst of our sins. That is a life well lived. That is fighting the good fight and finishing the race. Accept His grace. Respond with gratitude.

Then tell the world.

LET'S START WITH ONE. NAME ONE PERSON WHO YOU CAN TELL THAT GOD LOVES THEM NO MATTER WHAT.

..................................................................................................

..................................................................................................

..................................................................................................

PRAY THAT GOD WILL GIVE YOU THE COURAGE TO SHARE HIS MIND-BLOWING LOVE WITH OTHERS. PRAY THAT HIS GRACE IN YOU WILL OVERFLOW TO AT LEAST ONE PERSON.

# CONGRA-
# TULATIONS,
# ME!

NAME:

DATE:

SOMETHING I LEARNED ABOUT PAUL:

# I FINISHED THIS JOURNAL!

SOMETHING I LEARNED ABOUT GRACE

ONE WAY GRACE WILL HELP ME TO LIVE FREE

# WORKS CITED

1. 2 Corinthians 11:23-25 ESV

2. 2 Corinthians 11:26-28 ESV

3. 1 Timothy 1:15 NLT

4. "Adele Opens Up About Her Inspirations, Looks and Stage Fright." Rolling Stone. 28 Apr. 2011. <http://www.rollingstone.com/music/news/adele-opens-up-about-her-inspirations-looks-and-stage-fright-20120210?page=2>

5. "Rocky" http://www.rottentomatoes.com/m/1017776-rocky/reviews/?sort=-fresh

6. "Moldova"  http://en.wikipedia.org/wiki/Moldova

7. "Student Is Billionaire Overnight." Sky News.  23 Oct. 2008 <http://news.sky.com/story/642951/student-is-billionaire-overnight>

8. Acts 13:13-23 NLT

9. 2 Corinthians 1:20 ESV

10. Acts 13:26 NLT

11. Acts 13:38 NLT

12. Domart, Yves, Garet, Emmanuel.  "Lichtenberg Figures Due to a Lightning Strike ." New England Journal Of  Medicine. 23. Nov. 2000 <http://www.nejm.org/doi/full/10.1056/NEJM200011233432105>

13. Acts 13:34 NLT

14. "Billy Hayes (Writer)" <http://en.wikipedia.org/wiki/Billy_Hayes_(writer)>

15. "Juliane Koepcke" < http://en.wikipedia.org/wiki/Juliane_Koepcke>

16. Galatians 1:11-16 NLT

17. Smith, Sean. "Will Smith: Hollywood's Most Powerful Actor?" Neweek. 08 Apr. 2007 < http://www.newsweek.com/will-smith-hollywoods-most-powerful-actor-97639>

18. Ephesians 5:1-2 NLT

19. Acts 20:1-4 NLT

20. "Largest Rubber Duck Collection- World Record Set By Charlotte Lee." World Record Academy. 14 May 2010. < http://www.worldrecordacademy. com/collections/largest_rubber_duck_collection_world_record_set_by_ Charlotte_Lee_101696.htm>

21. "The 6,000 Barbie Doll Man Shows His Collection" NDT.TV < http://www. ntd.tv/en/news/world/asia-pacific/20130906/82586-the-6000barbie-doll-man-shows-collection.html>

22. "11 Weird Collections" Rounds.com < http://www.rounds.com/ blog/11-weird-collections/>

23. Philippians 2:1-2 NLT

24. Philippians 2:1-2 The Message

25. Gray, Emma. "Women in The Workplace: Most Women Look In The Mirror Eight Times A Day, Survey Shows." The Huffington Post. http://www. huffingtonpost.com/2012/05/14/women-workplace-look-in-mirror-8-times-a-day-survey_n_1515316.html

26. Philippians 2:3-4 NLT

27. Philippians 2:5 NLT

28. Ephesians 4:31-32 NLT

29. Romans 6:1-2 NLT

30. Acts 28:17-24 and 30-31 NLT

31. 2 Timothy 4:6-8 NLT

32. Auden, W H. "For The Time Being: A Christmas Oratorio." For the Time Being. London: Faber and Faber, 1945. Print.

33. Chappell, Bill. "Reduced To Her Knees, Marathoner Finish-es Race In A Crawl." NPR. http://www.npr.org/blogs/thet-wo-way/2015/02/17/386983481/reduced-to-her-knees-marathoner-finishes-race-in-a-crawl

34. Ellis, Samantha. "Humpback Whale Gives Thanks To Divers." Globalanimal. org 26 Nov. 2013. < http://www.globalanimal.org/2013/11/26/happy-thanksgiving-humpback-whale-gives-thanks-to-divers-for-rescuing-her/>

# ABOUT THE AUTHORS

## BEN CRAWSHAW

heads up content development for The Rocket Company, a church resourcing organization. He also leads the student initiative (XP3 Students and High School Camp) at the reThink Group. Previously Ben was the Creative Director of High School Ministry at North Point Community Church. He graduated from Lee University in Cleveland, TN, where he studied English and begged for food. In his free time, you can find Ben doing the Braves' Tomahawk Chop, watching non-horror movies, or eating Reese's Pieces. He and his wife Holly love living in their hometown of Cumming, GA. They have two daughters, Lilah and Esmae, and an unruly cat named Cupcake.

## JARED JONES

currently serves as the director of Student Ministries at Orangewood Church in Orlando, FL, where he lives with his wife, Sarah. When Jared isn't arguing with Florida fans about the superiority of the Georgia Bulldogs, he enjoys Netflix, cooking, and obsessing about the future of the Star Wars franchise. (Come on, Disney. Don't mess this up!). As a graduate of Liberty University and Reformed Theological Seminary, Jared is passionate about helping students find where their story and God's story intersect.